2000 EARLY ADVERTISING CUTS

Clarence P. Hornung

DOVER PUBLICATIONS, INC.
New York

Published in Canada by General Publishing Company, Ltd., 30 Lesmill Road, Don Mills Toronto, Ontario.
Published in the United Kingdom by Constable and Company, Ltd., 3 The Lanchesters, 162–164 Fulham Palace Road, London W6 9ER.

Bibliographical Note

2000 Early Advertising Cuts, published by Dover Publications, Inc., in 1995, is an abridged republication (the introductory essay, with its illustrations, has been omitted; the plate section is intact) of the third, revised edition (1956) of the *Pictorial Volume* of the two-volume work *Handbook of Early Advertising Art: Mainly from American Sources*, first published by Dover in 1953.

The publisher is indebted to the following persons for their assistance in preparing the Second Edition: Massey Trotter, librarian at the New York Public Library Print Room, who searched for new material for sections on holidays and mortised cuts. Paul H. Downing, consultant on equipage, Staten Island, N. Y., who supervised the compilation of Plates 103 through 115 on horse drawn vehicles. The notes for these plates, which appear in the Appendix, were also prepared by Mr. Downing. Cyril Nast, who loaned us the drawings of his father, Thomas Nast. The New York Historical Society for permission to reproduce material from the Landauer Collection. The Staff of the New York Public Library in general and the Photographic Division in particular, for their usual admirable, indispensable assistance on many different problems. Barrows Mussey and Ruth M. Canedy, who helped locate some Christmas illustrations. The Ford Motor Company, the Packard Motor Car Company, and the Studebaker Corporation for permission to use material in the automobile section.

DOVER *Pictorial Archive* SERIES

Library of Congress Cataloging-in-Publication Data

Hornung, Clarence Pearson.
  2000 early advertising cuts / by Clarence P. Hornung. — 4th ed.
      p.   cm. — (Dover pictorial archive series)
  Rev. ed. of: Handbook of early advertising art, mainly from American sources.
  Includes bibliographical references and index.
  ISBN 0-486-28843-9
    1. Commercial art—United States—History—19th century—Themes, motives.
  2. Commercial art—United States—History—20th century—Themes, motives.
  I. Hornung, Clarence Pearson. Handbook of early advertising art, mainly from American sources.   II. Title.   III. Series.
  NC998.5.A1H67   1995
  741.6′7′0973—dc20   95-6701
                                                                                              CIP

Manufactured in the United States of America
Dover Publications, Inc.
31 East 2nd Street
Mineola, N.Y. 11501

PREFACE TO THE FOURTH EDITION

2000 Early Advertising Cuts was formerly the Pictorial Volume of the *Handbook of Early Advertising Art: Mainly from American Sources*. The introductory chapter, with its accompanying illustrations, has been omitted in this new edition, which also features some minor repagination and corrections in the front matter and index. The plates, however, have not been altered in any way.

PREFACE TO THE THIRD, REVISED EDITION

The Pictorial Volume of the HANDBOOK OF EARLY ADVERTISING ART has been enlarged by the addition of sixteen plates of pictures taken from Trade Advertisements of the early 19th century. They were selected to give a clear portrayal of both the exteriors and interiors of retail and manufacturing establishments of this period. They also add to the available pictures of machines, instruments, carriages, dress, etc. All of the new material was photographed directly from original prints.
1956

The Publisher

PREFACE TO THE SECOND, REVISED EDITION

There has been a steady demand for a new printing of the HANDBOOK OF EARLY ADVERTISING ART, and the publisher has taken this opportunity to revise and expand the work along the lines of its greatest usefulness.

The HANDBOOK's greatest usefulness has been to working artists, printers, advertising agencies, and others in the graphic arts. Expansion and revision has therefore been made mainly with the needs of these practitioners in mind. Like the old typefounders' books from which it draws so much of its material, this book has become a source of cuts, illustrations, and typography. In this respect, it is a direct lineal descendant of the type specimen books of Johnson; MacKellar, Smiths and Jordan; and other "swipe chests" of the period rather than a treatise or history of these early works.

This new edition differs from the old in the following ways:

1. Expansion of the pictorial and typographical material has been so extensive as to necessitate two separate volumes. One is devoted exclusively to illustration, and the other to typography and typographical ornamentation.

2. Almost every cut has been rephotographed from source material in order to achieve greater clarity. If certain deficiencies in clarity are still present, they reflect the well-worn quality of the original cuts.

3. Sections that have proved especially useful have been greatly expanded, and new sections have been added. Many holidays lend themselves to nostalgic presentation, and therefore, new cuts have been added to the sections on food and drink (Thanksgiving) and patriotic emblems (Independence Day). The section of Christmas cuts appears for the first time. In gathering material for the Christmas section, it was necessary to use sources other than the typefounders' catalogues because the growth of Christmas is a twentieth-century phenomenon. Christmas illustrations appear to have played a very minor role in advertising and selling in the nineteenth century. However, the publisher feels that in going to non-advertising sources, he is following in the footsteps of the nineteenth-century typefounders who readily appropriated cuts from spelling books and periodicals for similar purposes.

CONTENTS

THE PLATES

The illustrations shown on the following plates have been taken, for the most part, from type specimen books representative of the nineteenth century. A careful inspection of these volumes reveals that the cuts not only appear repeatedly in subsequent issues, but in the pages of several different foundries as well. A listing of these source books will be found in the Appendix, together with notes on the plates.

1

2

3

4

5

6

1

2

3

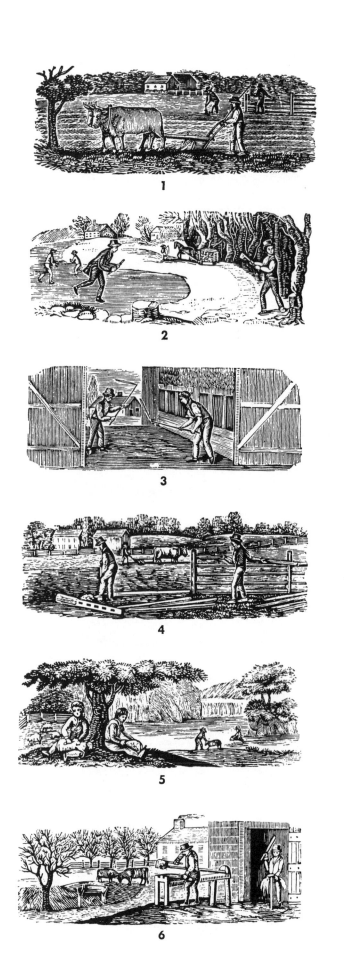

1

2

3

4

5

6

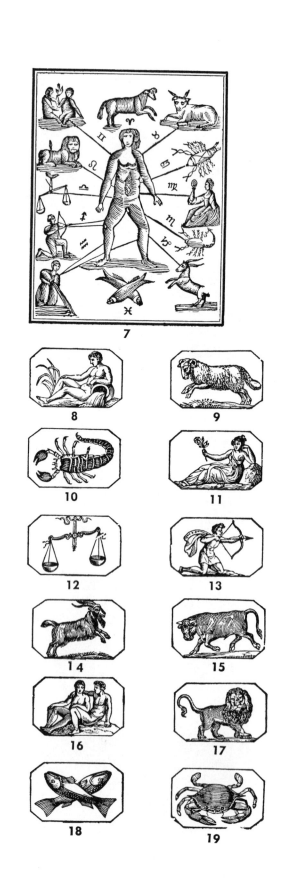

7

8

9

10

11

12

13

14

15

16

17

18

19

1

2

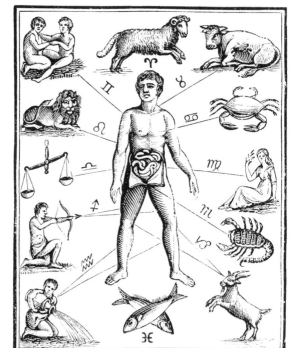

4

3

5

1

2

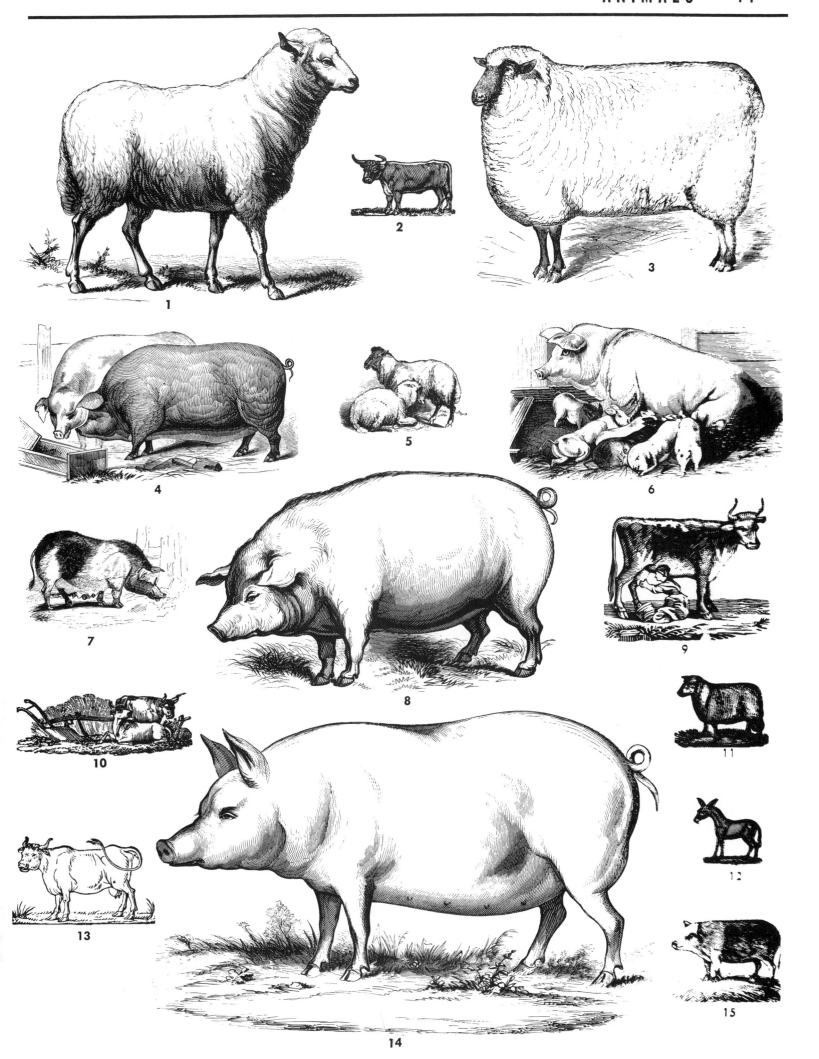

1

2

3

4

5

6

7

8

9

10

11

12

13

14

15

16

17

1

2

3

4

5

6

7

8

9

10

11

12

13

1

2

3

4

5

6

7

8

9

10

11

12

13

14

1

2

3

4

5

1

2

3

4

5

6

7

8

9

1

2

3

4

5

6

1

2

3

4

5

6

7

8

9

10

11

12

13

14

1

2

3

4

5

6

7

8

9

10

11

12

13

14

15

16

17

1

2

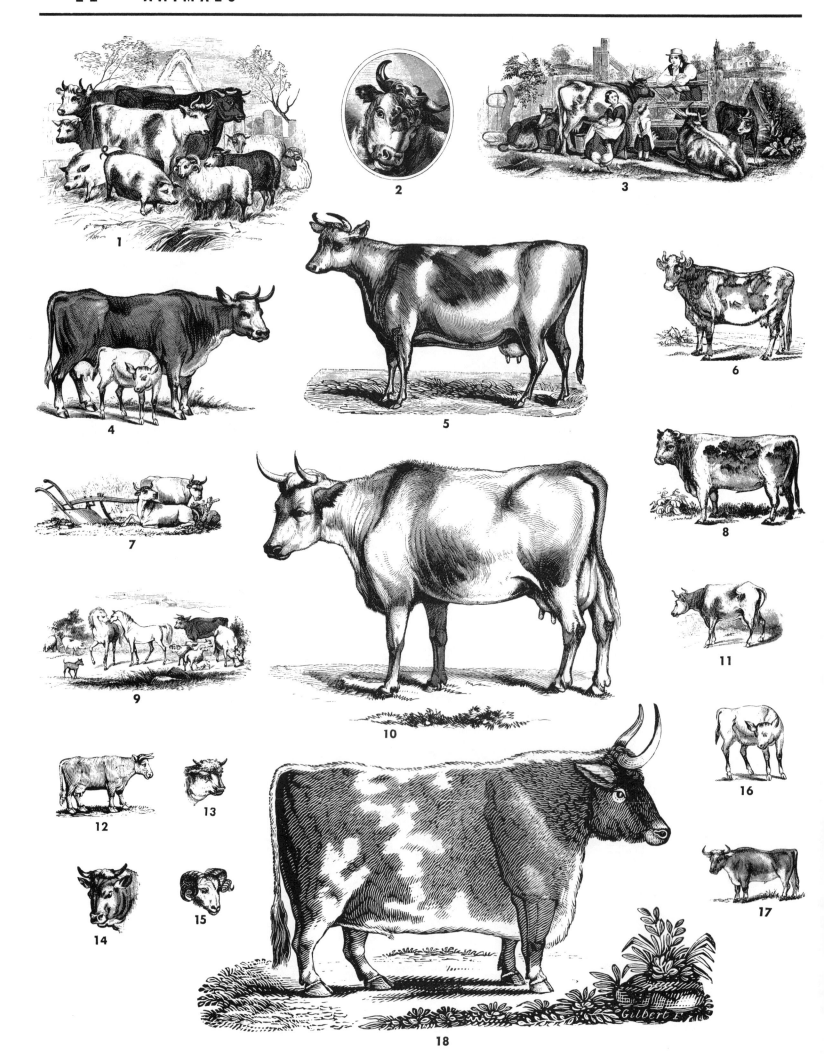

1

2

3

1

2

3

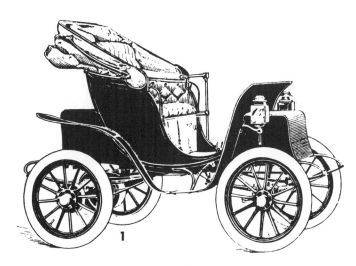

1

1911
Packard Eighteen
Landaulet

2

3

1

2

3

4

1

2

3

4

1

2

3

4

1

2

3

4

5

6

7

8

9

10

1

2

3

4

5

6

7

8

9

10

2

1

3

4

5

6

7

8

9

10

11

2

3

1

4

5

6

7

8

9

10

11

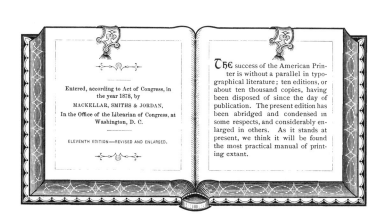

COMPACT
Book of Specimens
OF
Printing Types.

Entered, according to Act of Congress, in
the year 1878, by
MACKELLAR, SMITHS & JORDAN,
In the Office of the Librarian of Congress, at
Washington, D. C.

ELEVENTH EDITION—REVISED AND ENLARGED.

THE success of the American Printer is without a parallel in typographical literature; ten editions, or
about ten thousand copies, having
been disposed of since the day of
publication. The present edition has
been abridged and condensed in
some respects, and considerably enlarged in others. As it stands at
present, we think it will be found
the most practical manual of printing extant.

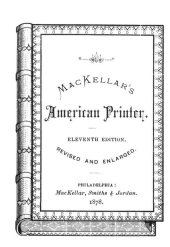

MACKELLAR'S
American Printer.

ELEVENTH EDITION.
REVISED AND ENLARGED.

PHILADELPHIA:
MacKellar, Smiths & Jordan.
1878.

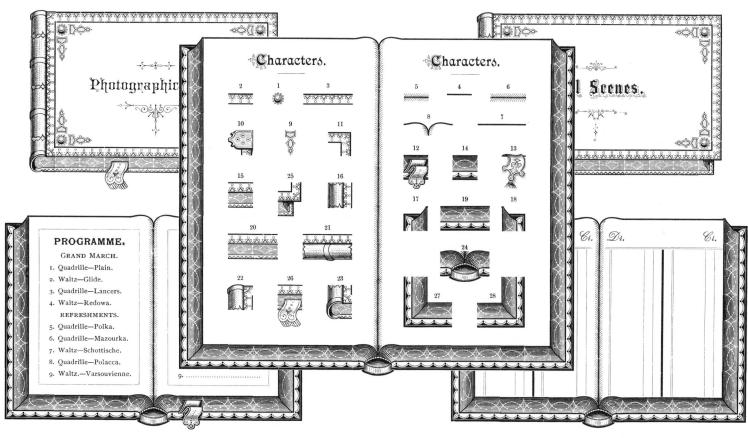

Photographic

Characters.   Characters.

PROGRAMME.
GRAND MARCH.
1. Quadrille—Plain.
2. Waltz—Glide.
3. Quadrille—Lancers.
4. Waltz—Redowa.
REFRESHMENTS.
5. Quadrille—Polka.
6. Quadrille—Mazourka.
7. Waltz—Schottische.
8. Quadrille—Polacca.
9. Waltz.—Varsouvienne.

Scenes.

Cr.   Dr.   Cr.

TYPE-FOUNDERS and
others are respectfully
notified that we reserve all
rights in our new Cuts, bearing a copyright notice, and
any infringement on the
same will be legally con-
tested.

ELEVENTH
BOOK OF SPECIMENS
MACKELLAR, SMITHS & JORDAN.

This new Border Series
admirably fills a place
hitherto unoccupied among
the appliances of the Typographic Art. We present it
to the craft as another evi-
dence of our desire to place
within their reach every
means of diversifying the
appearance of their skilful
handiwork.

MacKellar, Smiths & Jordan.

1

2

3

4

5

6

7

8

1

2

3

4

5

6

7

1

2

3

4

1

2

3

4

5

6

7

8

9

10

11

12

13

14

15

16

17

18

1

2

3

1

2

3

4

5

1

2

3

1

2

3

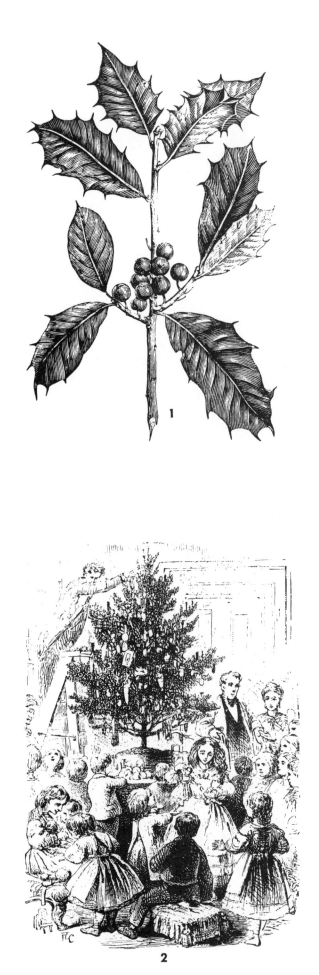

1

2

3

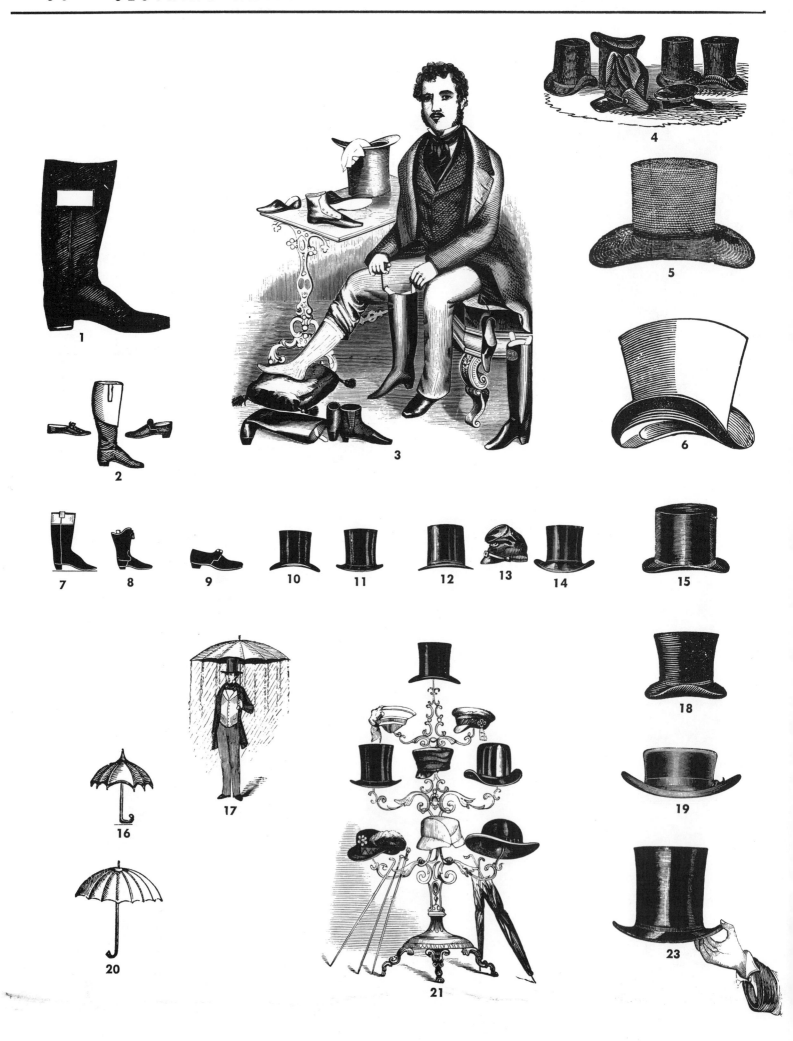

1

2   3   4

5   6

7

LETTERS PATENT
E. CHESTERMAN,
NEW-YORK.

COMMERCE

FREEDOM

AMERICA

E PLURIBUS UNUM

1

2

1

2

3

4

5

6

7

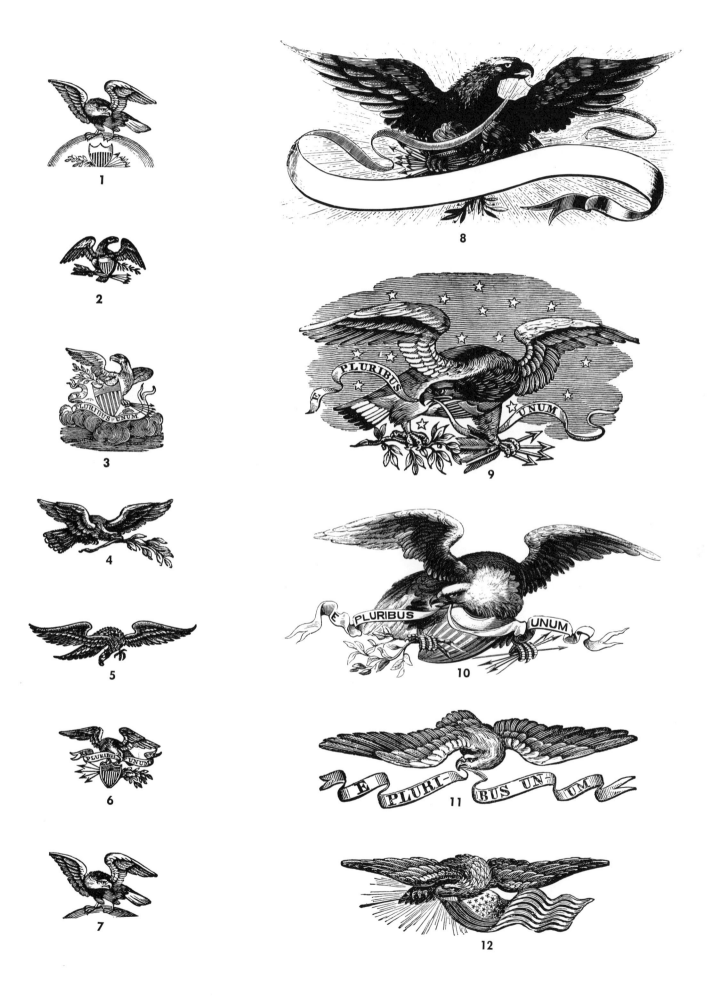

THE CONSTITUTION FOREVER.

THE UNION AND

L. JOHNSON & CO.

1

2

3

4

5

1

2

3

4

5

6

7

8

1

2

3

4

5

6

1

3

2

4

5

6

7

8

9

1

2

3

4

5

6

7

8

9

10

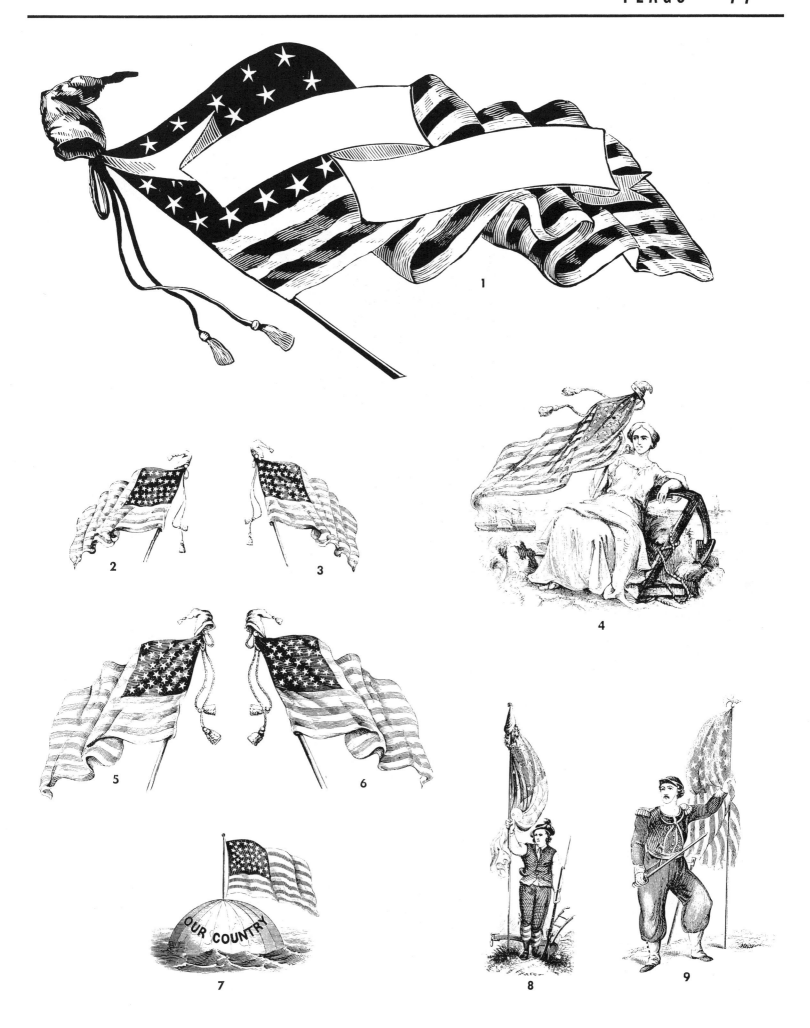

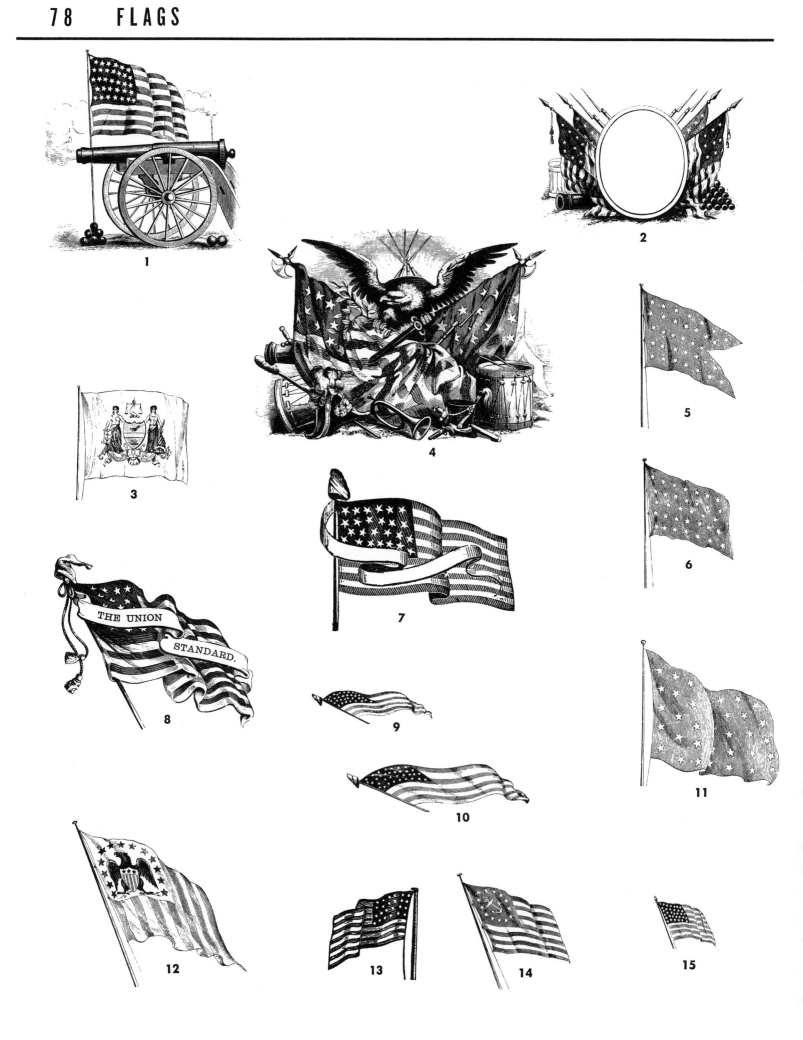

1

2

3

4

5

6

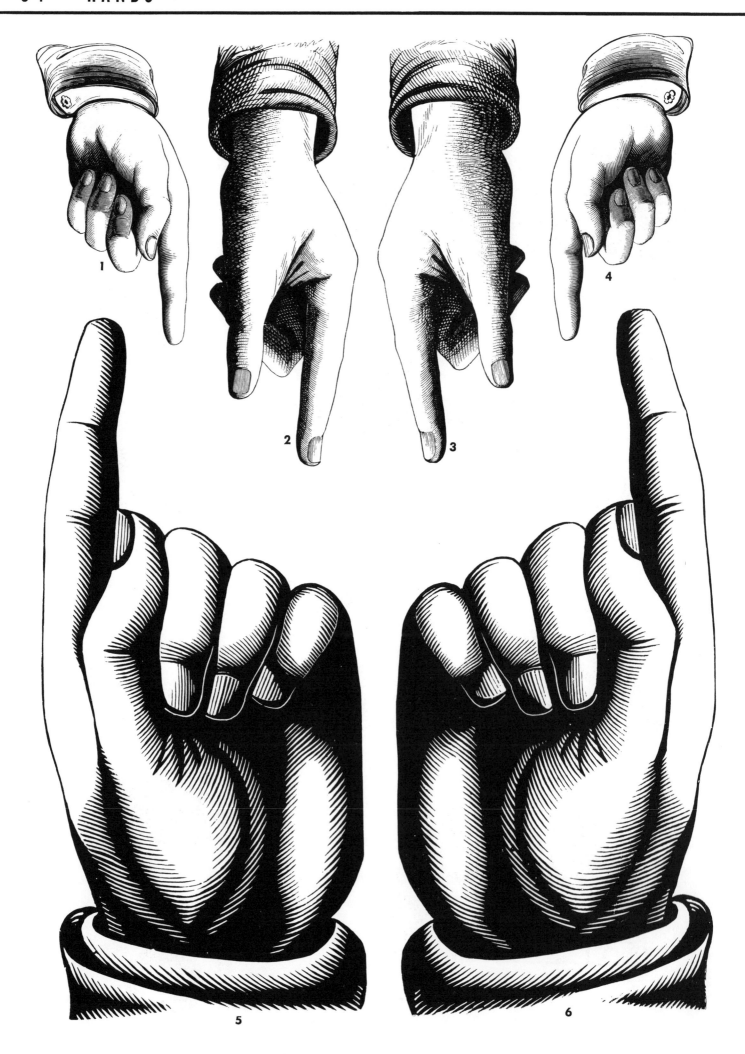

Index Corners

These Index Corners
are Electrotyped,

and Blocked on
Solid Metal Bodies.

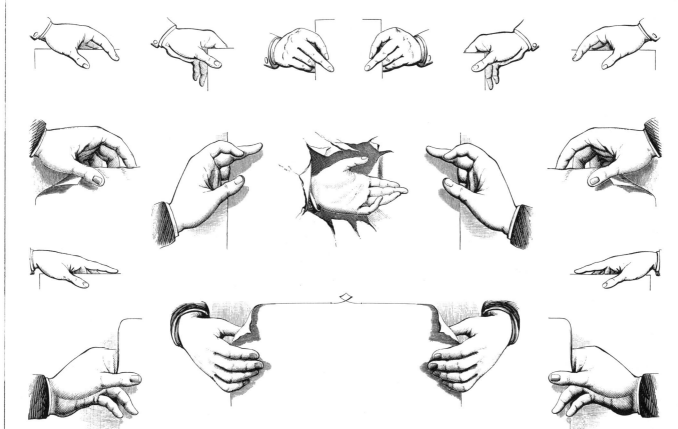

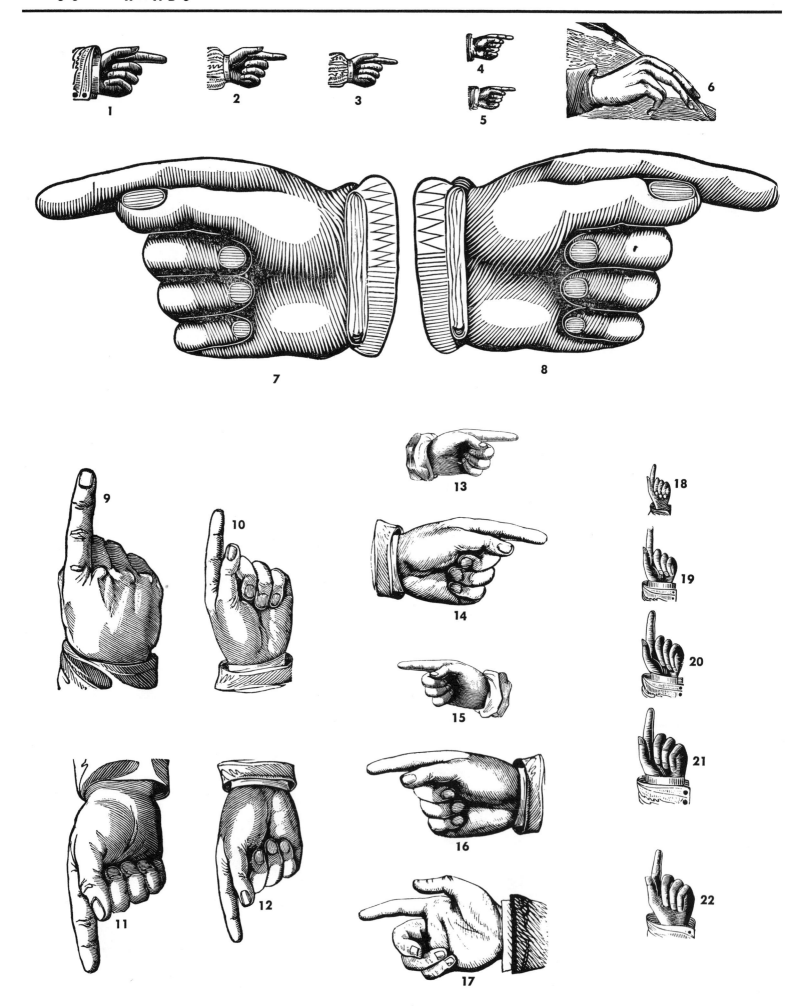

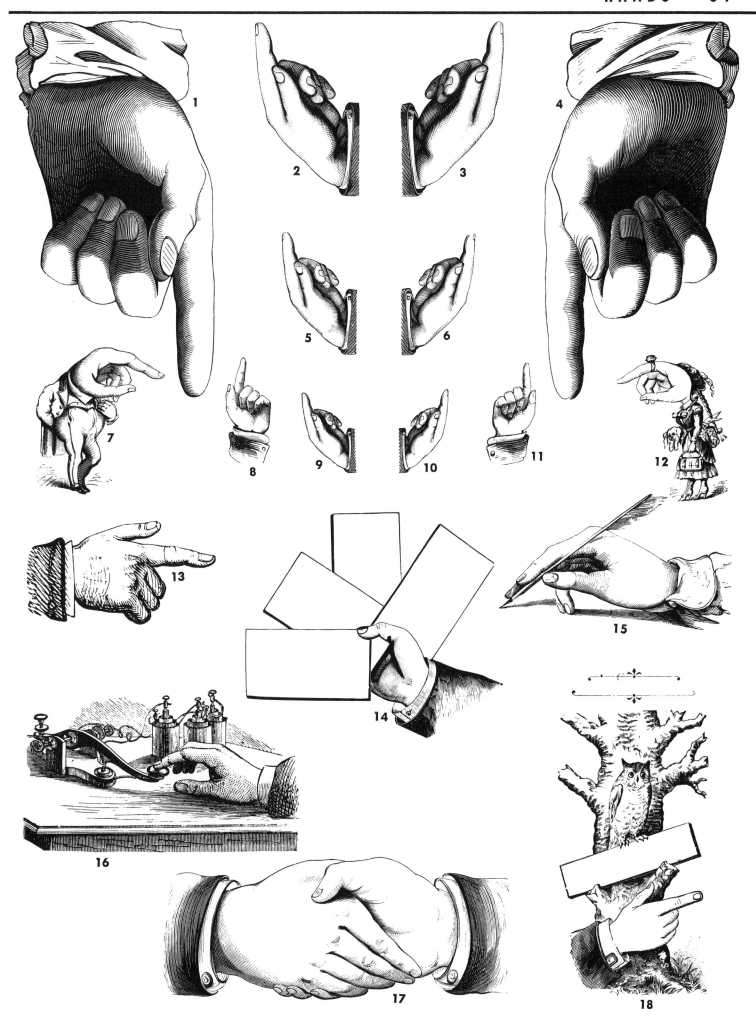

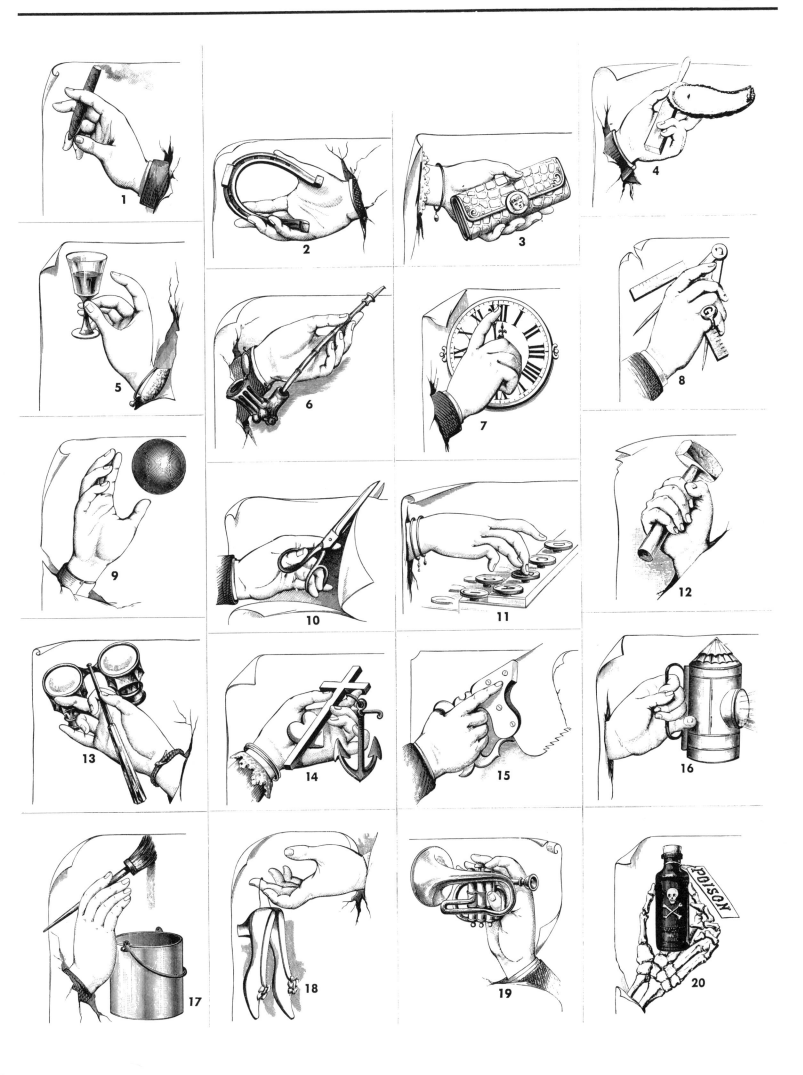

1

2

3

4

5

6

1

2

3

4

5

6

7

1

2

1

2

3

1

2

L. JOHNSON & CO.

1

2

1

2

1

2

3

4

5

1

2

3

4

5

1

2

3

1

2

3

4

5

6

7

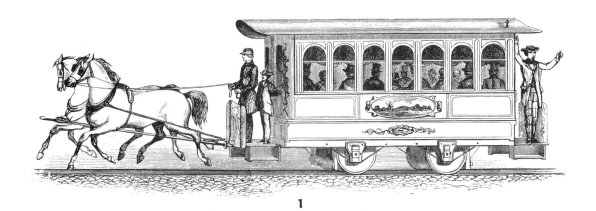

1

2

3

1

2

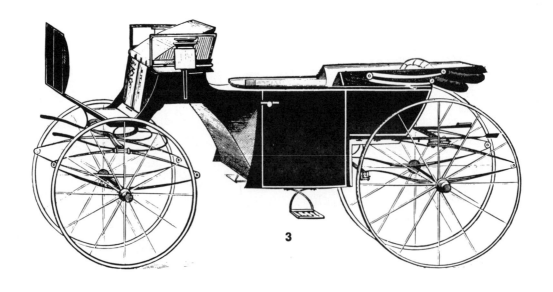

3

1

2

1

2

1

2

3

4

1

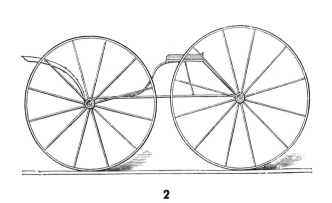

2

3

4

1

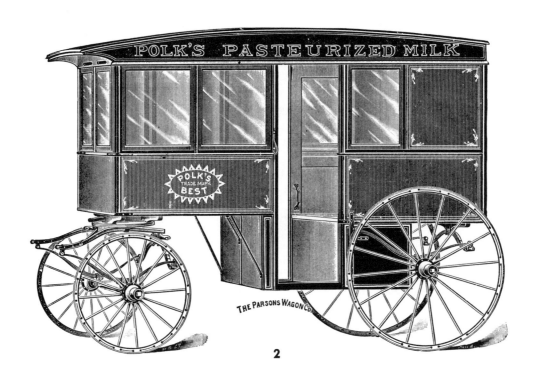

2

1

2

3

1

2

3

4

5

6

7

8

1

2

1

2

3

4

5

6

7

8

9

10

11

12

13

14

15

16

17

18

19

20

21

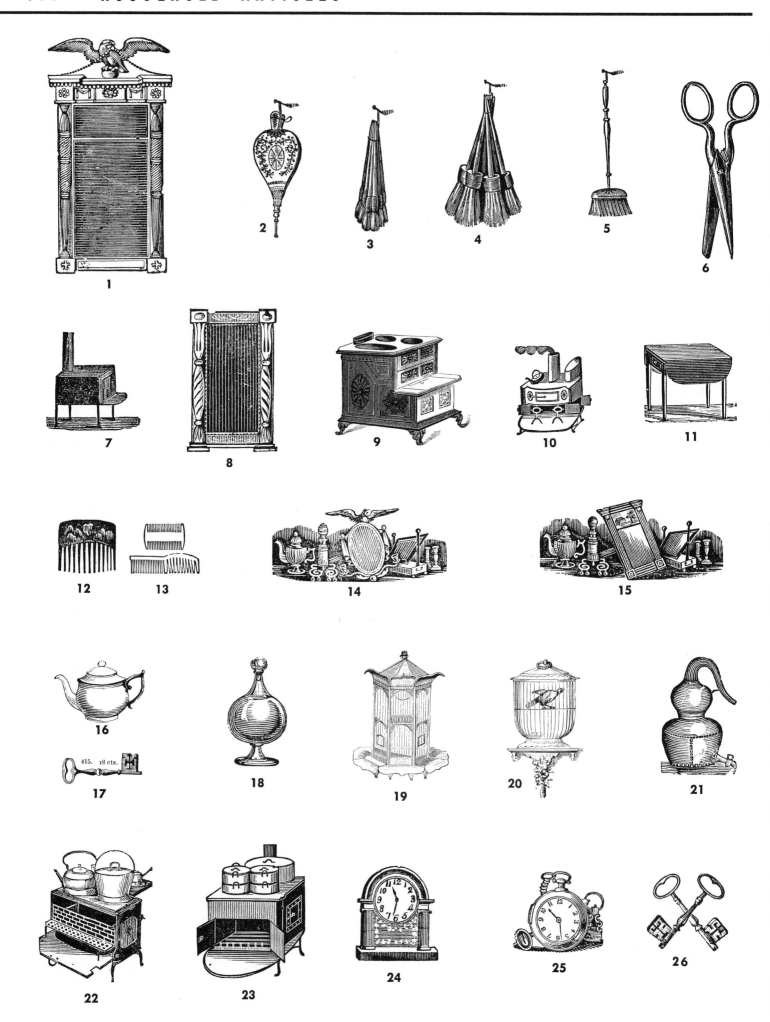

1

2

3

4

5

6

7

8

1

2

3

4

5

6

7

1

2

3

4

5

6

7

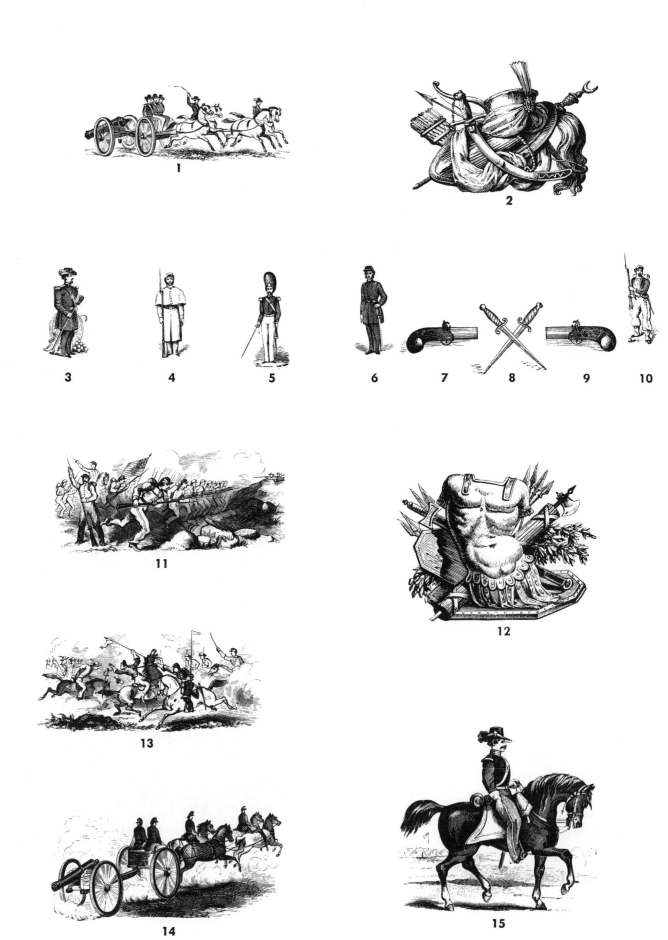

1

2

3

4

5

6

7

8

9

10

11

12

13

14

15

1

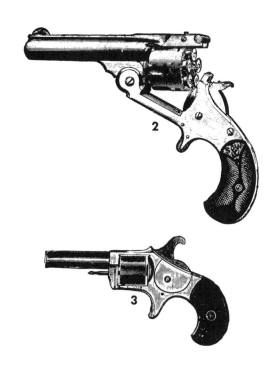

2

3

4

5

6

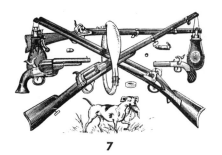

7

1

2

3

4

5

6

7

8

9

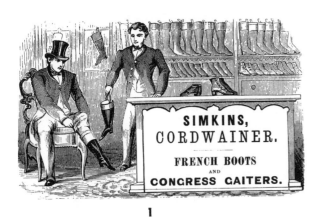

1

2

3

4

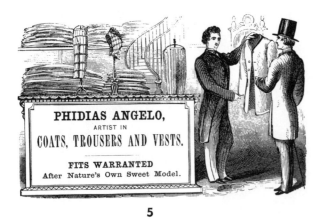

5

6

7

8

1

2

3

4

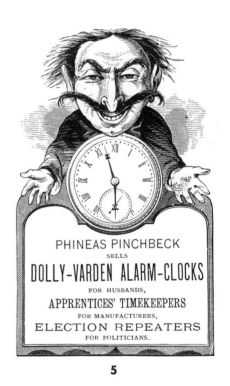

5

6

7

8

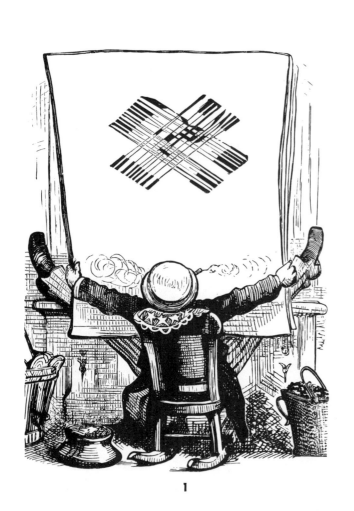

1

2

3

4

1

2

3

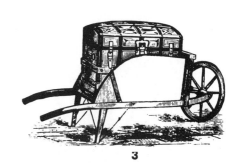

4

GREAT LAND ENTERPRISE AT LUNAVILLE!

ROUSING OPPORTUNITY!

Five Hundred Acres on the Sunny Side of the Moon
to each Subscriber.

WITH LOTS OF ROCK FOR BUILDING PURPOSES!

When one half the stock is taken, an Atmospheric Engine will be erected in the crater of Popocatapetl to furnish refined air to the settlers, and a Steam Squirt will be placed on Goat Island to play water on the Moon, so that the inhabitants will have always enough—never too much, and never too little; thus avoiding the drouths and drenchings to which the earth's people are liable. Balloons also will be provided to start daily from different available points on the earth.

NOW IS THE TIME TO SUBSCRIBE!

5

1

2

3

4

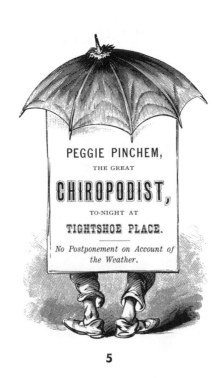

5

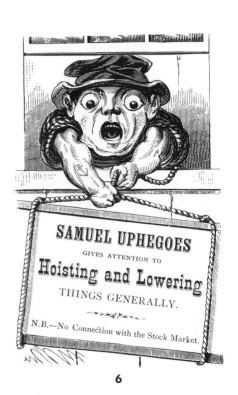

6

1

2

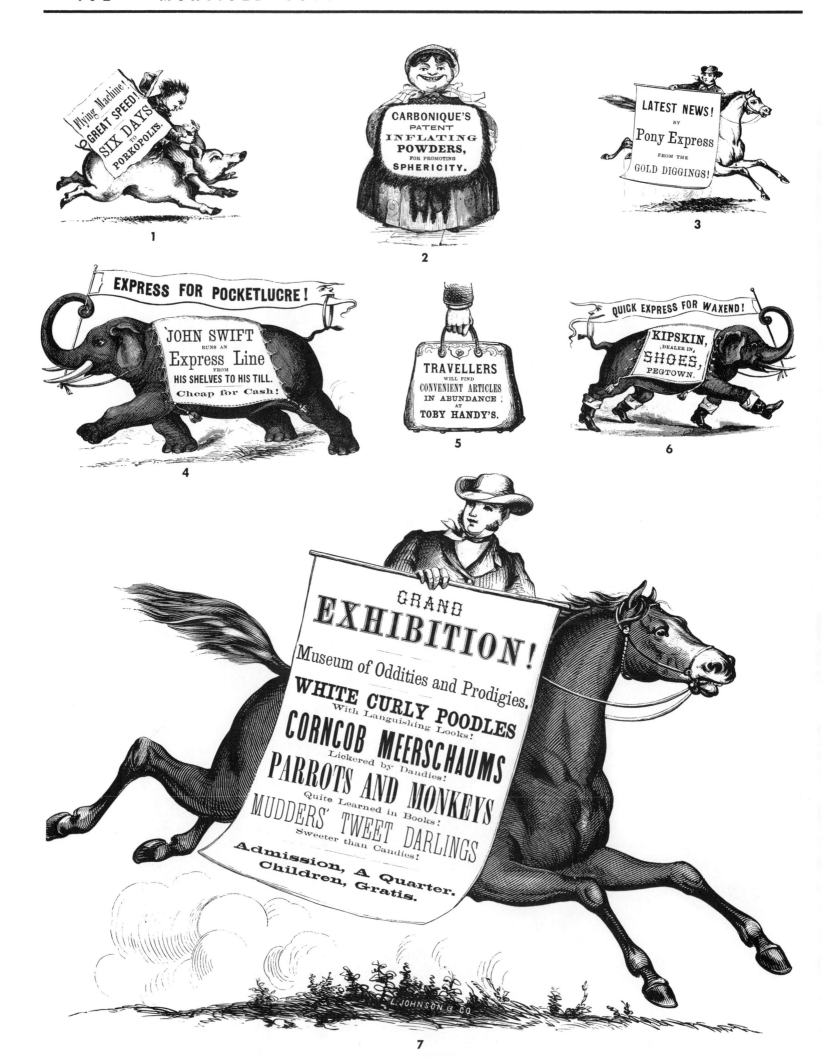

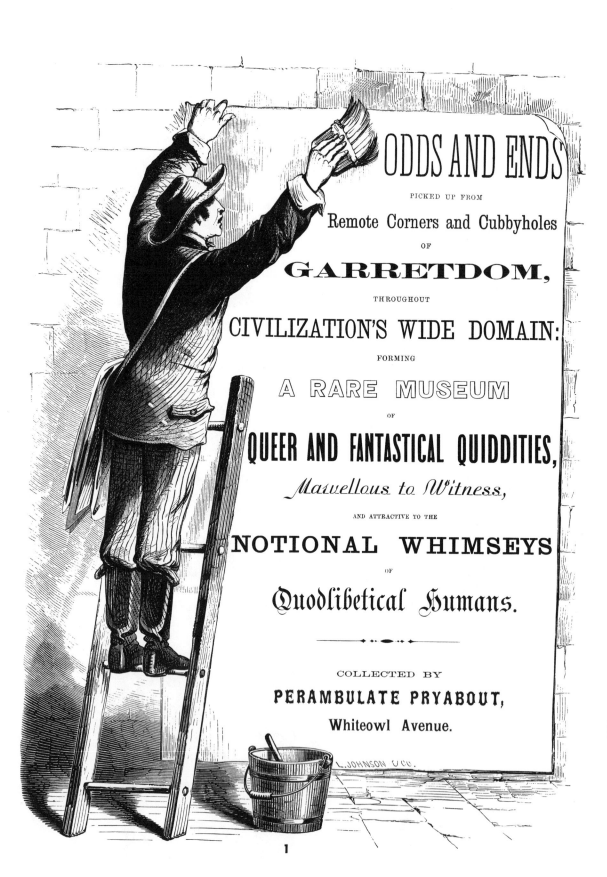

ODDS AND ENDS

PICKED UP FROM

Remote Corners and Cubbyholes

OF

GARRETDOM,

THROUGHOUT

CIVILIZATION'S WIDE DOMAIN:

FORMING

A RARE MUSEUM

OF

QUEER AND FANTASTICAL QUIDDITIES,

Marvellous to Witness,

AND ATTRACTIVE TO THE

NOTIONAL WHIMSEYS

OF

Quodlibetical Humans.

COLLECTED BY

PERAMBULATE PRYABOUT,

Whiteowl Avenue.

1

CAMERA & SUN,

Photographic Artists.

240 Attic Row,

PICTUREVILLE.

2

TAKE PARTICULAR NOTICE.

3

Notice to Travellers.

FURNITURE

REMOVED

During the Owner's Absence.

Proceeds Equally Divided by

Masculine Kleptomaniacs.

4

1

2

3

4

1

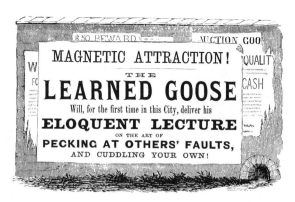

2

3

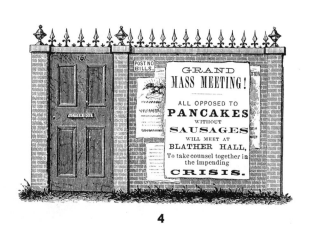

4

5

6

1

2

3

4

5

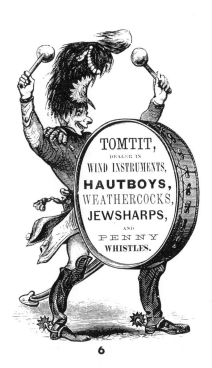

6

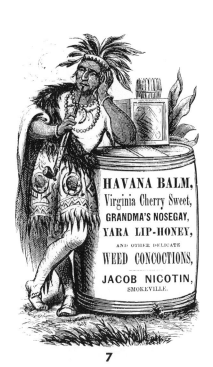

7

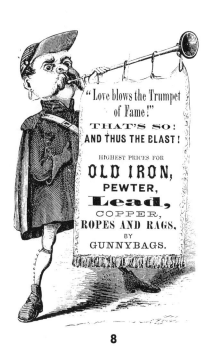

8

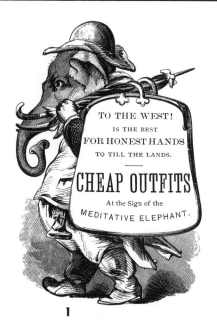

TO THE WEST!
IS THE BEST
FOR HONEST HANDS
TO TILL THE LANDS.

CHEAP OUTFITS

At the Sign of the
MEDITATIVE ELEPHANT.

1

All the Fair,
With Beaming Eye and Curly Hair,
SING IN PRAISE OF THE

ACME

HAIR DYE.

*It will curl straight hair, and
straighten curled hair.*

2

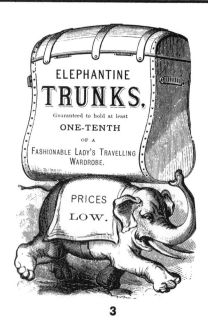

ELEPHANTINE
TRUNKS,
Guaranteed to hold at least
ONE-TENTH
OF A
FASHIONABLE LADY'S TRAVELLING
WARDROBE.

PRICES
LOW.

3

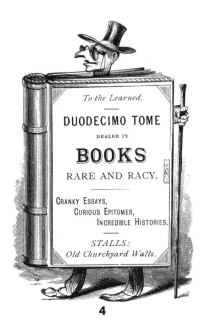

To the Learned.

DUODECIMO TOME

DEALER IN

BOOKS

RARE AND RACY.

CRANKY ESSAYS,
CURIOUS EPITOMES,
INCREDIBLE HISTORIES.

STALLS:
Old Churchyard Walls.

4

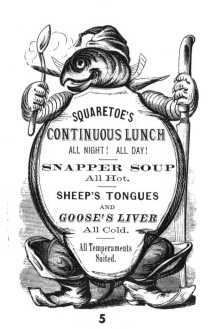

SQUARETOE'S
CONTINUOUS LUNCH
ALL NIGHT! ALL DAY!
SNAPPER SOUP
All Hot.
SHEEP'S TONGUES
AND
GOOSE'S LIVER
All Cold.

All Temperaments
Suited.

5

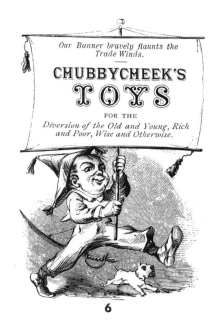

*Our Banner bravely flaunts the
Trade Winds.*

**CHUBBYCHEEK'S
TOYS**

FOR THE

*Diversion of the Old and Young, Rich
and Poor, Wise and Otherwise.*

6

*They sing it in the parlours,
It is whistled all about,
They play it on hand-organs,*
THAT

STUBB'S

BLACKING

IS THE

BEST SHINER OUT.

Only 10 Cents a Box.

7

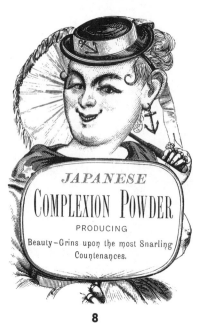

JAPANESE
COMPLEXION POWDER
PRODUCING
Beauty-Grins upon the most Snarling
Countenances.

8

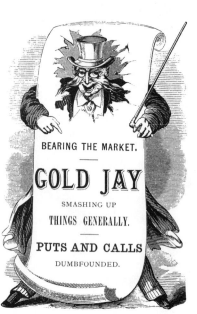

BEARING THE MARKET.

GOLD JAY

SMASHING UP

THINGS GENERALLY.

PUTS AND CALLS

DUMBFOUNDED.

9

1

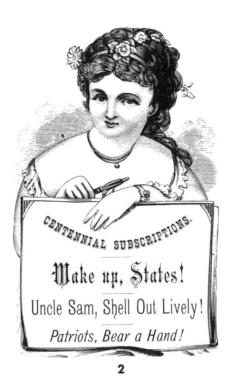

2

3

4

5

6

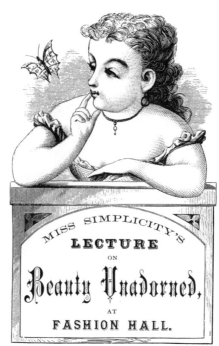

REFLECTIONS

ON THE

Morality of Founders

WHO CRIB

OUR ORIGINAL CUTS.

1

MISS SIMPLICITY'S

LECTURE

ON

Beauty Unadorned,

AT

FASHION HALL.

2

ROAD TO HEALTH.

Up in the Morning Early.

HERE SHE GOES, THERE SHE GOES.

3

EVERLASTING LOVE-KNOTS

SECURELY TIED BY

PARSON SILVERTONGUE,

CATHEDRAL PORCH,

BLUEBEARDTOWN.

4

1

2

3

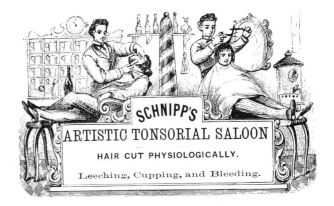

4

5

6

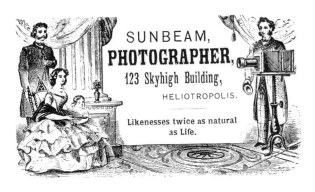

7

8

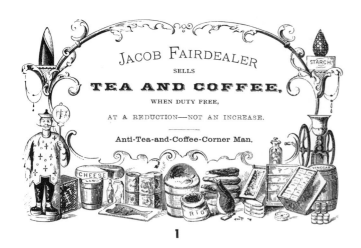

1

2

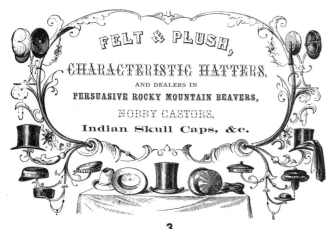

3

4

5

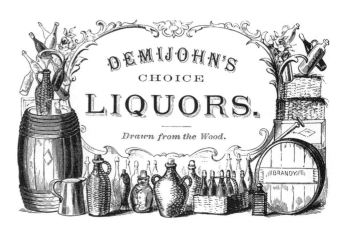

6

7

8

Universal Intelligencer.

VOL. XXIV.

APRIL, 1871.

No. 13.

HIGHLY INTERESTING!

LOVERS OF GENTLE CONSORTS,

Wives and Children,

Rightminded Brothers, Devoted Sisters,

FOND GRANDPAPAS,

Child-Spoiling Grandmammas,

MAIDEN AUNTIES,

GENEROUS UNCLES,

EXPECTANT NIECES,

AND

HAIRBRAINED NEPHEWS,

ALL,

Without Distinction of Age or Sex,

WILL FIND

KEENER'S CORN-SALVE

UNRIVALLED!

L. JOHNSON & CO.

1

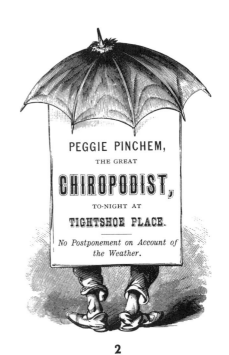

PEGGIE PINCHEM,

THE GREAT

CHIROPODIST,

TO-NIGHT AT

TIGHTSHOE PLACE.

No Postponement on Account of
the Weather.

2

All-Hallow-Eve.

NOCTURNAL RANGERS,

TAKE

WARNING!

No Signs to be Misplaced
Hereafter.

Growler Watchem.

3

FLORAL EXHIBITION.

4

Squatter Sovereignty.

Priority of Claim

NO, YOU DON'T, PUSSY!

The Old Bone of Contention.

5

1

2

3

4

5

6

7

8

9

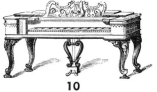

10

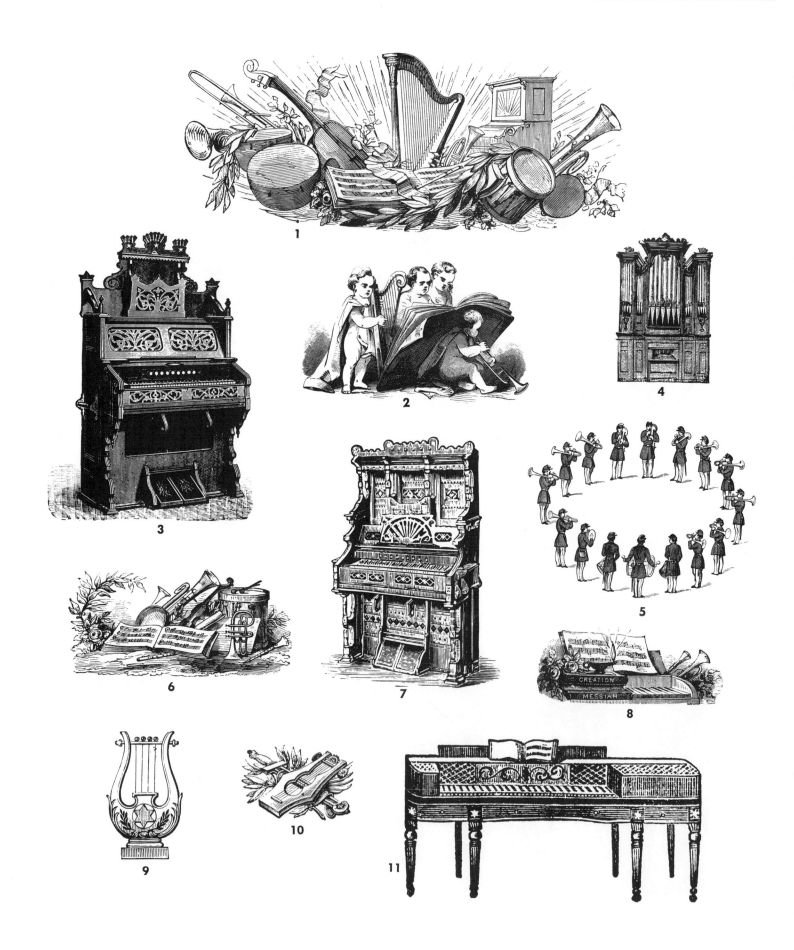

1

2

3

4

5

6

7

8

9

10

11

1

2

4

3

5

6

1

2

3

4

5

6

Let her bang, ye Heroes!

Victory is Ours!

1

2

3

4

1

2

3

4

5

6

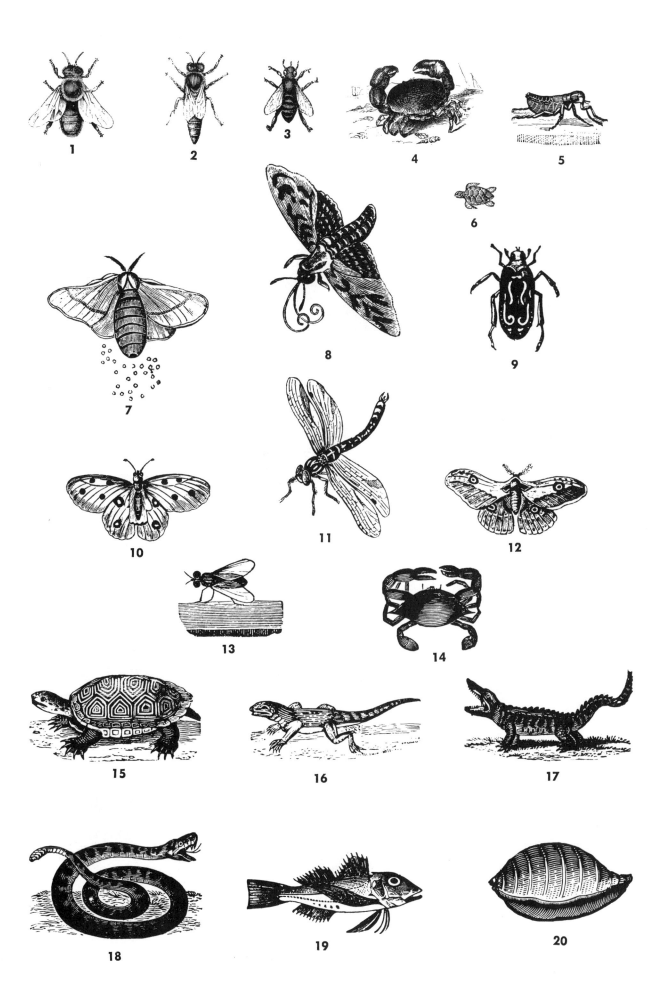

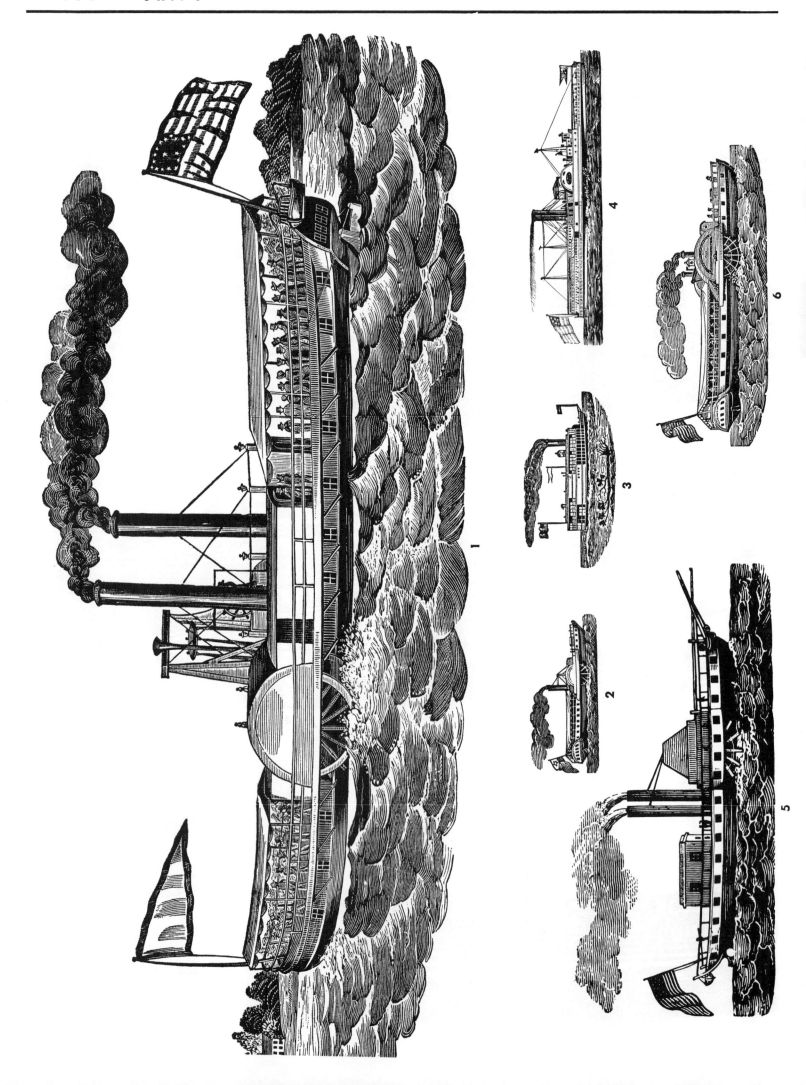

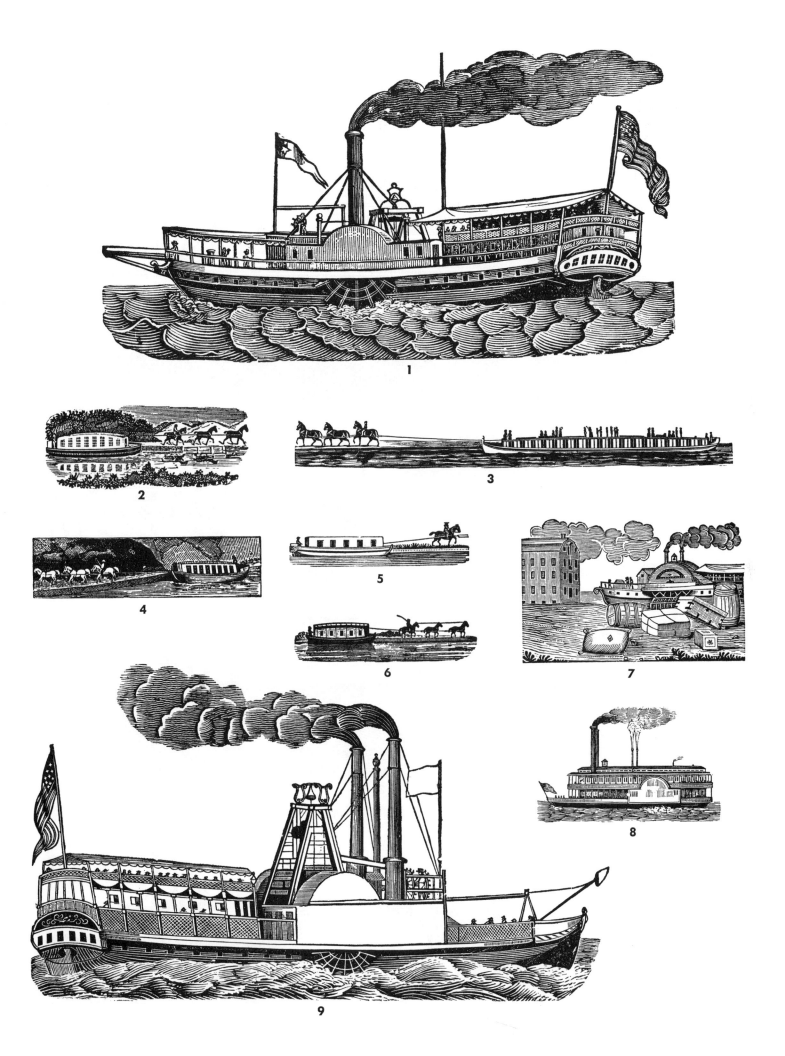

1

2

3

4

5

6

1

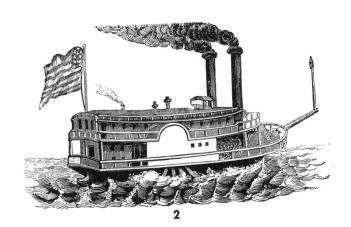

2

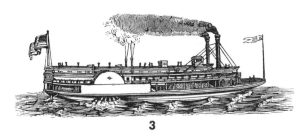

3

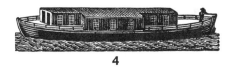

4

5

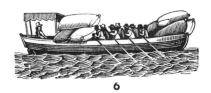

6

7

8

9

10

11

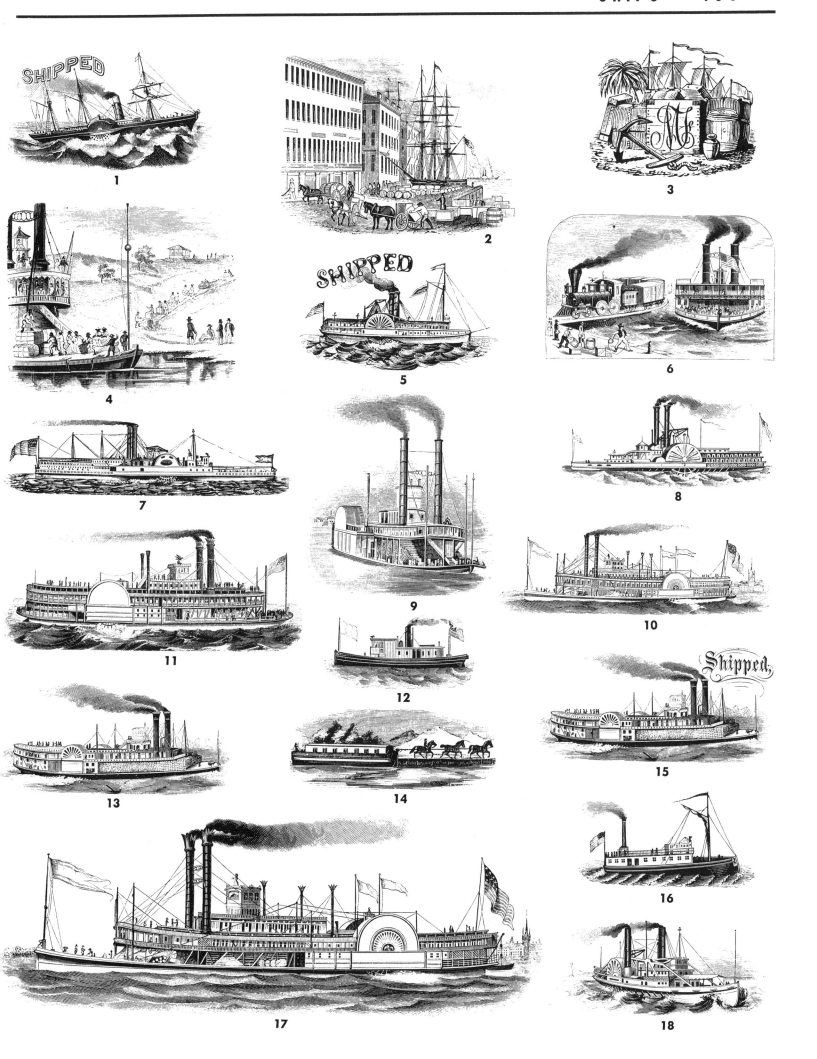

1

2   3   4

5

6

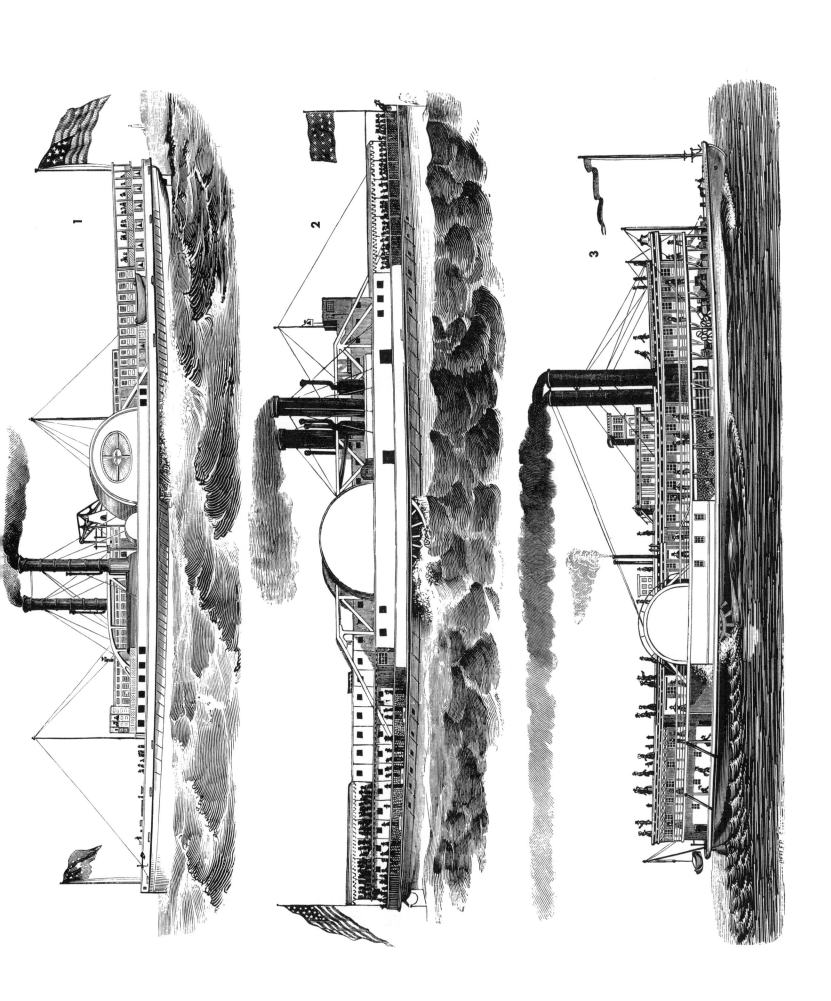

1

2

3

4

5

6

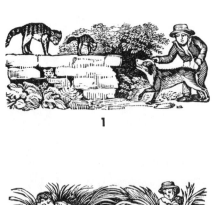

1

2

4

5

6

7

8

9

10

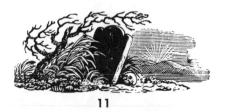

11

12

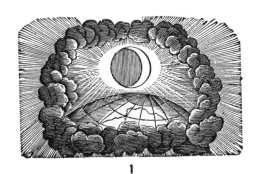

1

2

3

4

5

6

7

1

2

3

4

5

6

1

2

3

4

5

6

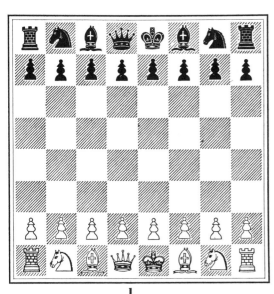

1

2

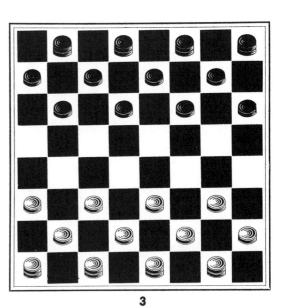

3

4

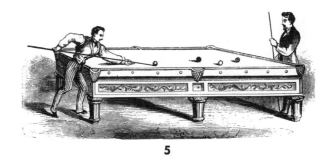

5

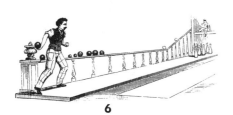

6

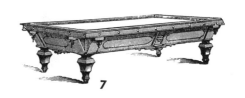

7

8

9

10

1

2

3

4   5

6

7

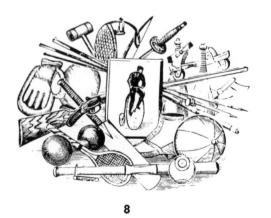

8

1

2

3

4

5

6

1

2

3

4

5

6

1

2

3

4

5

6

2

3

4

1

5

6

7

8

9

10

1

2

3

4

5

6

1

2

3

4

5

6

7

8

9

10

11

12

13

14

15

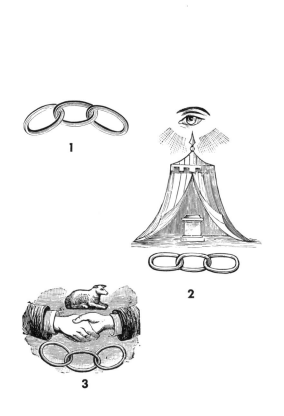

1

2

3

4

7

5

6

8

9

1

2

3

4

5

6

7

8

1

4

2

3

5

6

7

8

9

MILLINER.

MUSIC-DEALER.

NOTION-DEALER.

FURRIER.

GUNSMITH.

HATTER.

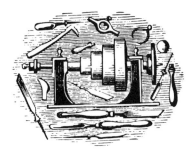

TURNER.

OPTICIAN.

FISHING-TACKLE.

TOBACCONIST.

TOY-DEALER.

TRUNK-MAKER.

BAKER.

WHEELWRIGHT.

WIRE-WORKER.

MINER.

CROCKERY.

TOBACCONIST.

HATTER.

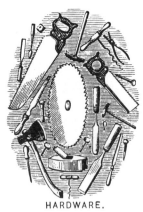

HARDWARE.

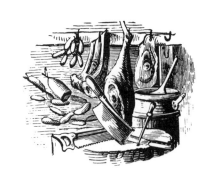

VICTUALLER.

DRUGGIST.

FARMER.

FLOUR-DEALER.

TAILOR.

TALLOW-CHANDLER.

TEA-DEALER.

STATIONER.

STEAM-ENGINE.

STOVE-MAKER.

PEN-DEALER.

PICKLES AND PRESERVES.

SADDLER.

SHIP-BUILDER.

SHIP-CHANDLER.

SHOE-FINDER.

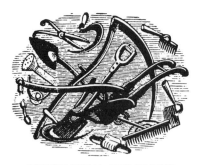

AGRICULTURAL IMPLEMENTS.

APOTHECARY.

ARTIFICIAL FLOWERS.

BASKET-MAKER.

BELL-HANGER.

BLACKSMITH.

BREWER.

BRICKLAYER.

BRUSH-MAKER.

CARPENTER.

CARRIAGE-BUILDER.

CEDAR-COOPER.

1

2

3

4

5

6

1

2

3

4

5

6

1

2

3

4

5

6

1

2

3

4

5

6

1

2

3

4

5

6

1

2

3

4

5

6

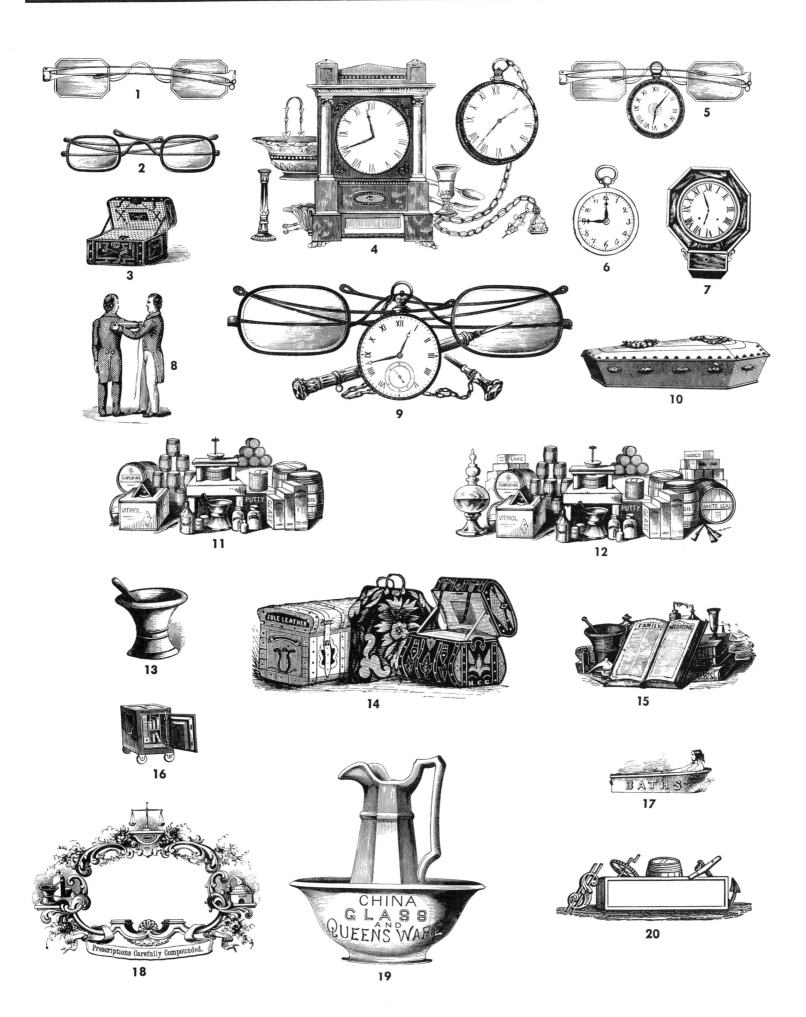

1

2

3

4

5

6

7

8

1

2

1

2

3

UMBRELLA-MAKER.

UNDERTAKER.

UPHOLSTERER.

SHOEMAKER.

STATIONER.

TEA-DEALER.

LIQUOR-DEALER.

MACHINIST.

PAINTER.

PAPER-HANGER.

PAWNBROKER.

PERFUMER.

PHOTOGRAPHER.

PIANO-MAKER.

PLUMBER.

PRINTER.

RESTAURANT.

SASH-MAKER.

SCALE-MAKER.

SEWING MACHINE.

HOSIER.

JEWELLER.

LAMP-MAKER.

CABINET-MAKER.

DENTIST.

LIQUOR-DEALER.

CHAIR-MAKER.

COMB-DEALER.

MARBLE-WORKER.

LOCKSMITH.

LUMBER-DEALER.

MACHINIST.

CHINA-WARE.

CLOCK AND WATCH-MAKER.

COAL-DEALER.

SHELL-FISH DEALER.

TINSMITH.

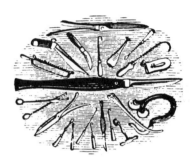

SURGICAL INSTRUMENTS.

SHOEMAKER.

BAKER.

BLINDS AND SHADES.

CONFECTIONER.

COPPERSMITH.

CUTLER.

DRY GOODS.

FARRIER.

FISH-DEALER.

FLORIST.

FLOUR-DEALER.

FRAME-MAKER.

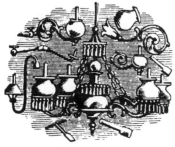

GAS-FITTER.

GENTLEMEN'S FURNISHER.

GROCER.

HAIR-DRESSER.

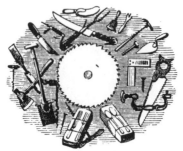

HARDWARE.

HARNESS-MAKER.

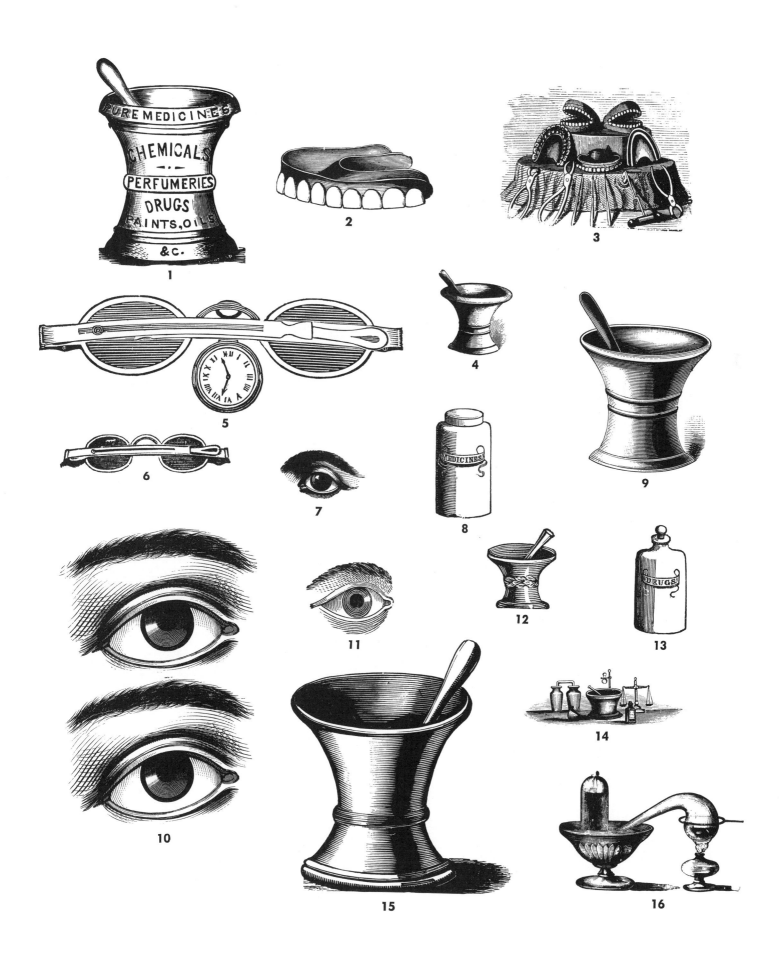

1

2

3

4

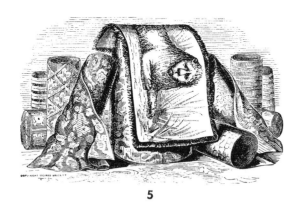

5

6

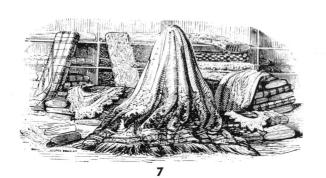

7

8

1

2

3

4

5

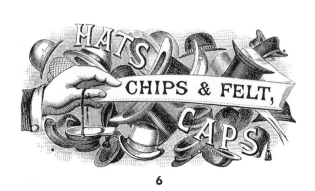

6

7

1

2

3

4

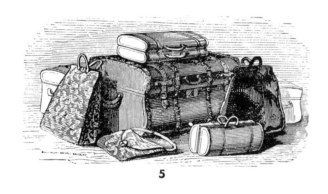

5

6

7

8

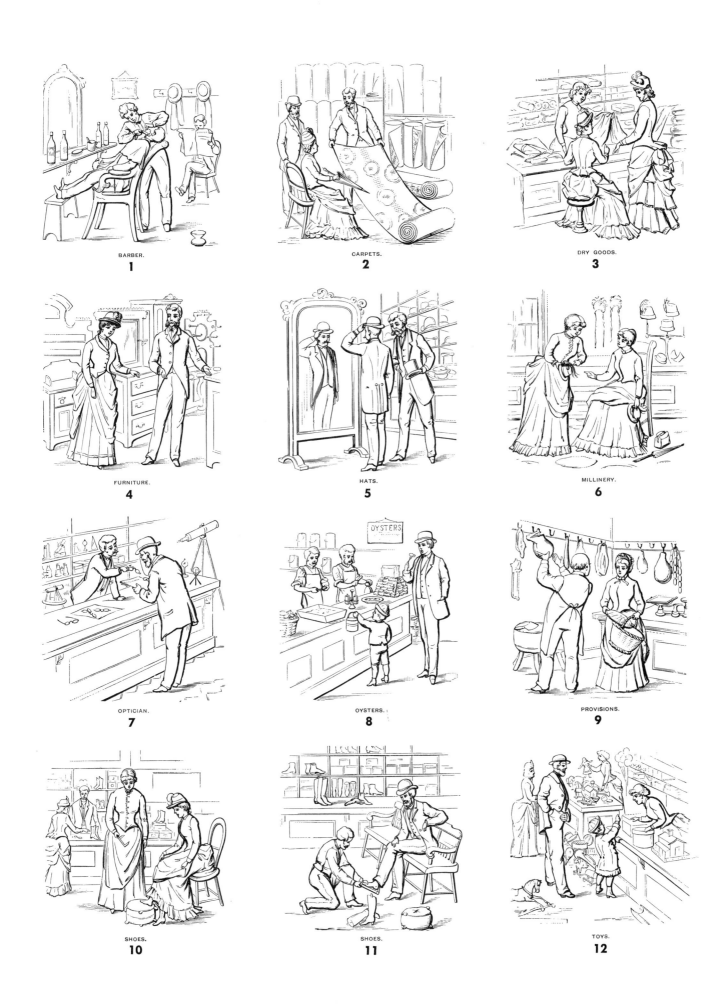

1

2

HARDWARE

3

4

5

6

FRESH TEAS.

7

8

9

10

GENUINE TEAS.

1

2

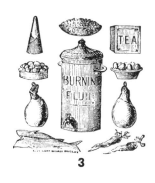

3

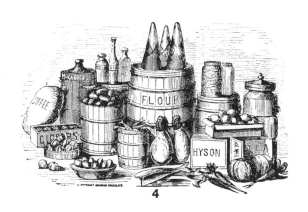

4

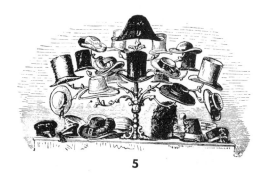

5

6

7

8

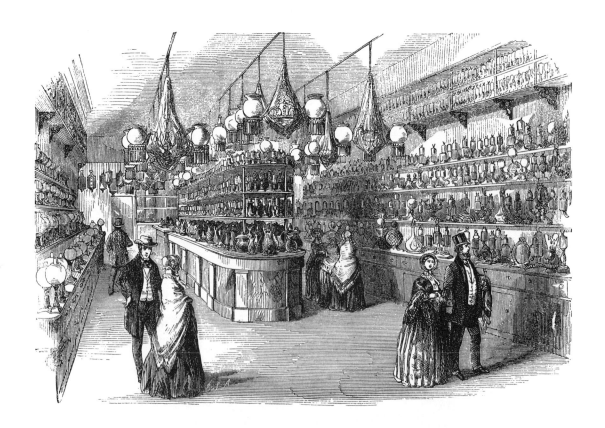

Manufacturer of and Dealer in

FLUID AND OIL CHANDELIERS,

DEALERS IN ALL KINDS OF

IRON AND STEEL,

WILLIAM WHITE,

PRINTER TO THE STATE,

COUNTING ROOM.

PRESS ROOM.

BOOK, NEWSPAPER, JOB, CARD AND ORNAMENTAL

PRINTER,

CORNER OF SPRING LANE & DEVONSHIRE STREET,

BOSTON, MASS.

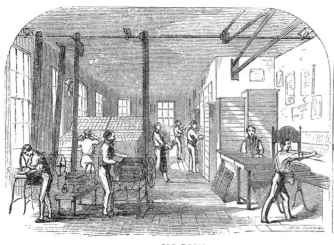

JOB ROOM

COMPOSITION ROOM.

OAK HALL CLOTHING HOUSE,

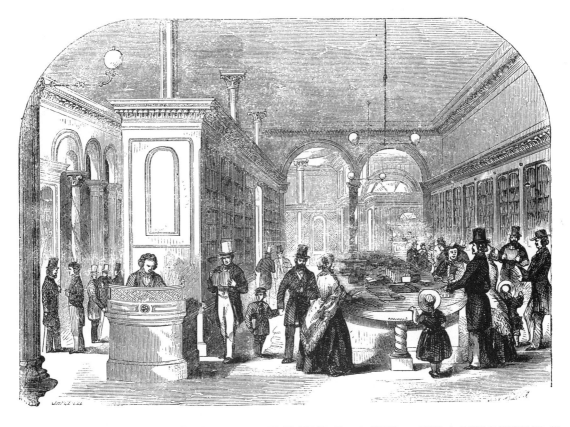

PUBLISHERS, BOOKSELLERS TRAND STATIONERS,

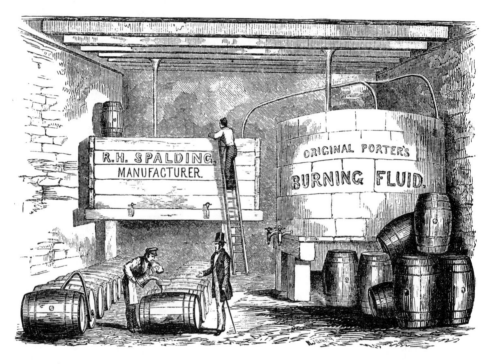

THE MOST COMPLETE ESTABLISHMENT IN THE UNITED STATES.

Alievi Enrico,

Riding Master.

THE BOSTON RIDING ACADEMY,

Era Works, Atlantic Docks, Brooklyn.

MANUFACTORY OF

GWYNNE'S PUMPING ENGINE,

SARGENT HARLOW, & Co.

SINGER'S SEWING MACHINES,

BROAD CLOTHS, CASSIMERES,

HARD AND SOFT COAL,

JOHN GOVE & COMPANY'S CLOTHING HOUSE,

UNITED STATES HOTEL, PHILADELPHIA,
C. J. MACLELLAN, PROPRIETOR.

BLAKE'S PATENT
FIRE-PROOF PAINT,

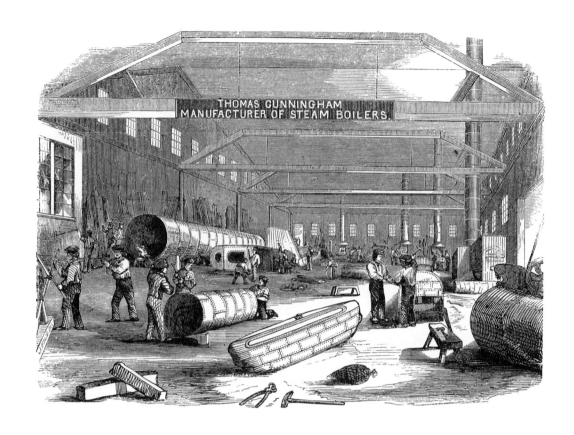

T. CUNNINGHAM, Manufacturer of Low & High Pressure Steam Boilers, of every description, Ships' Tanks, Coal Bunkers, Gasometers, &c. &c.

WATER STREET, Near Warren Bridge, Charlestown, Mass.

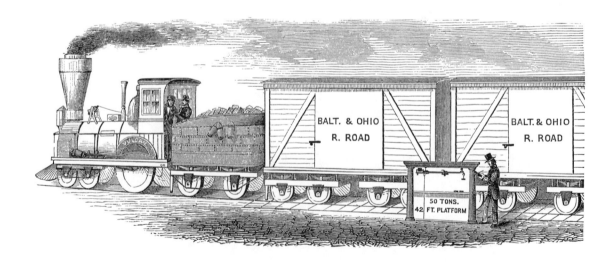

ALL KINDS OF
OMNIBUSES
MANUFACTURED BY
JOHN STEPHENSON
NEW-YORK.

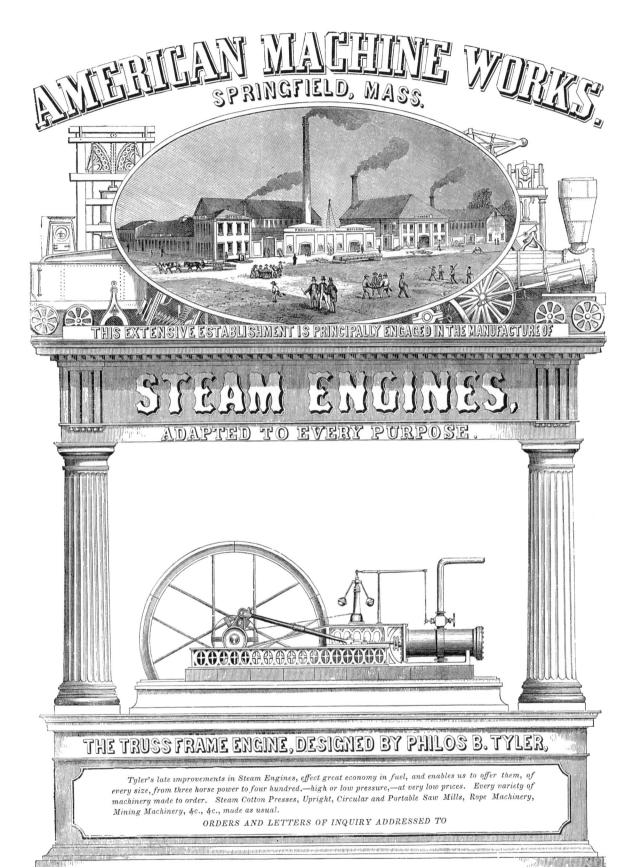

AMERICAN MACHINE WORKS.

SPRINGFIELD, MASS.

THIS EXTENSIVE ESTABLISHMENT IS PRINCIPALLY ENGAGED IN THE MANUFACTURE OF

STEAM ENGINES,

ADAPTED TO EVERY PURPOSE.

THE TRUSS FRAME ENGINE, DESIGNED BY PHILOS B. TYLER,

Tyler's late improvements in Steam Engines, effect great economy in fuel, and enables us to offer them, of every size, from three horse power to four hundred,—high or low pressure,—at very low prices. Every variety of machinery made to order. Steam Cotton Presses, Upright, Circular and Portable Saw Mills, Rope Machinery, Mining Machinery, &c., &c., made as usual.

ORDERS AND LETTERS OF INQUIRY ADDRESSED TO

PHILOS B. TYLER, PRES.^T

37 E

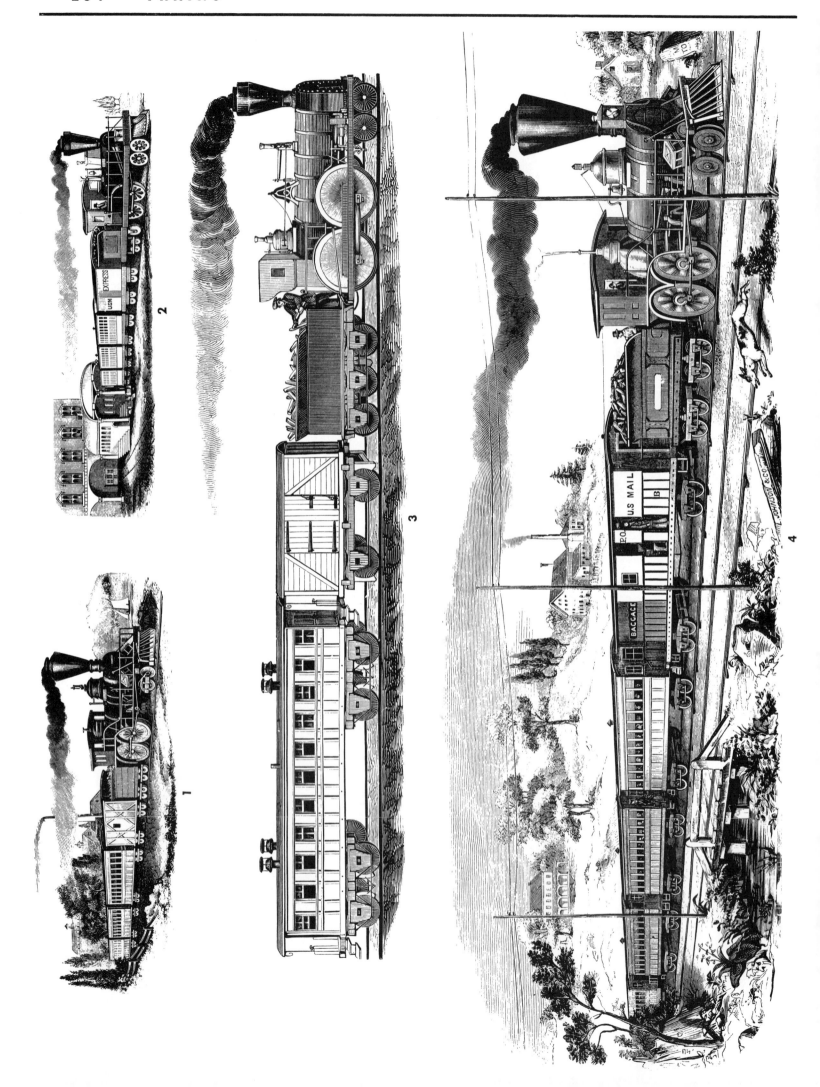

1

2

3

4

5

6

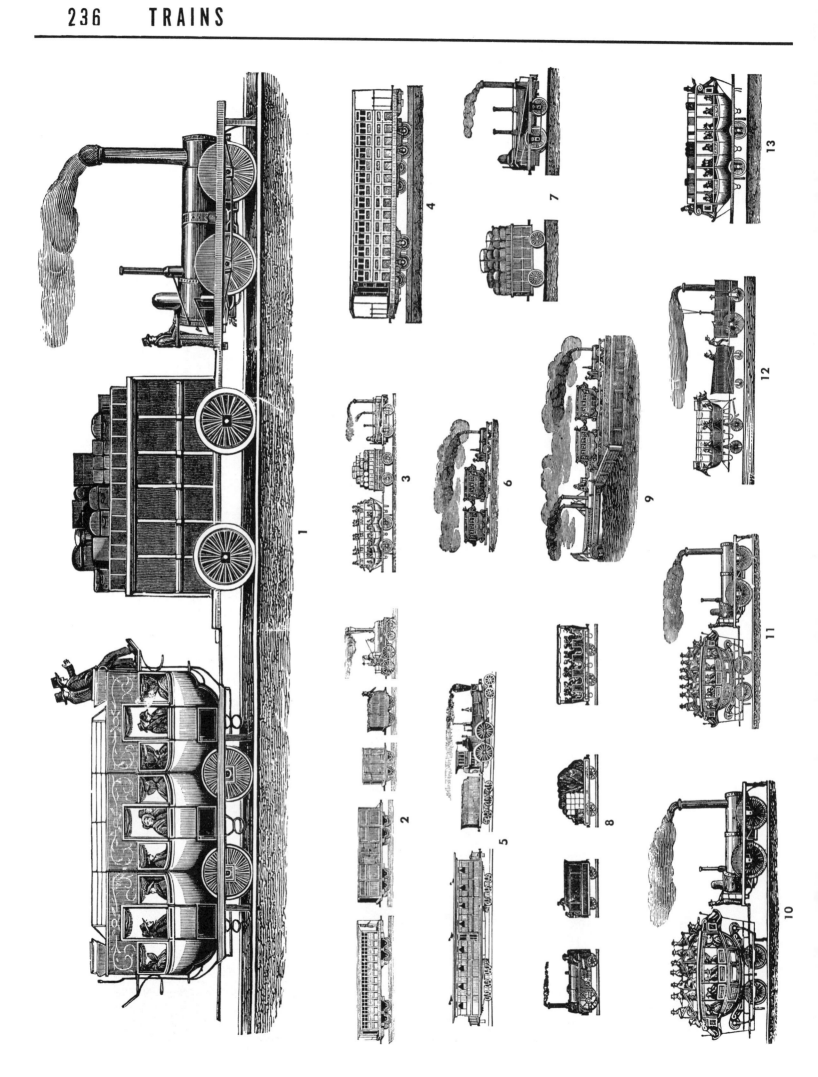

NOTES ON THE PLATES

Plate 12. ANIMALS. *Fig. 1*, Narwhal; *Fig. 2*, Zebra; *Fig. 3*, Vicuña; *Fig. 4*, Jaguar; *Fig. 5*, Polar Bear; *Fig. 6*, Hippopotamus; *Fig. 7*, Wolf; *Fig. 9*, Coati-mundi; *Fig. 10*, Whale; *Fig. 11*, Rabbits; *Fig. 12*, Rhinoceros; *Fig. 13*, Sheep; *Fig. 14*, Turtle; *Fig. 15*, Wildcat; *Fig. 16*, Tapir; *Fig. 17*, Tiger.

Plate 13. ANIMALS. *Fig. 1*, Dromedary; *Fig. 2*, Ant eater; *Fig. 3*, Beaver; *Fig. 4*, Cat; *Fig. 5*, Whalebone whale; *Fig. 6*, Reindeer; *Fig. 7*, Bear; *Fig. 8*, Leopard; *Fig. 9*, Kangaroo; *Fig. 10*, Lynx; *Fig. 11*, Fox; *Fig. 12*, Giraffe; *Fig. 13*, Ibex.

Plate 14. ANIMALS. *Fig. 1*, Bull; *Fig. 2*, Gazelle; *Fig. 3*, Bull; *Fig. 4*, Fox; *Fig. 5*, Goat; *Fig. 6*, Deer; *Fig. 7*, Kangaroo; *Fig. 8*, Bobcat; *Fig. 9*, Elephant; *Fig. 10*, Pig; *Fig. 11*, Horse; *Fig. 12*, Lion; *Fig. 13*, Antelope; *Fig. 14*, Gnu.

Plate 16. ANIMALS. *Fig. 1*, Cow; *Fig. 2*, Bear; *Fig. 4*, Bobcat; *Fig. 5*, Dromedary; *Fig. 6*, Sheep; *Fig. 7*, Donkey; *Fig. 8*, Bison; *Fig. 9*, Lion.

Plate 17. ANIMALS. *Fig. 1*, Racoon; *Fig. 2*, Deer and Dogs; *Figs. 3, 4*, Donkey; *Fig. 5*, Racoon; *Fig. 6*, Dog.

Plate 18. ANIMALS. *Fig. 2*, Tiger; *Fig. 3*, Elk; *Fig. 10*, Bear; *Fig. 11*, Lion; *Fig. 12*, Rat; *Fig. 13*, Bison.

Plate 19. ANIMALS. *Fig. 1*, Bison; *Fig. 2*, Donkey; *Fig. 3*, Cow; *Fig. 4*, Goat; *Fig. 5*, Elk; *Fig. 6*, Leopard; *Fig. 7*, Ibex; *Fig. 8*, Goat; *Fig. 9*, Zebra; *Fig. 10*, Antelope; *Fig. 11*, Moose; *Fig. 12*, Camel; *Fig. 13*, Walrus; *Fig. 14*, Monkey; *Figs. 15, 16*, Elephant; *Fig. 17*, Racoon.

Plate 23. AUTOMOBILES. *Fig. 1*, H. Mueller Mfg. 1896; *Fig. 2*, Locomobile 1918; *Fig. 3*, Pope-Toledo 1907.

Plate 24. AUTOMOBILES. *Fig. 1*, Packard 1908; *Fig. 2*, Molini 1911; *Fig. 3*, Packard 1913.

Plate 25. AUTOMOBILES. *Fig. 1*, Pope-Waverly 1907; *Fig. 3*, Overland 1908 H.A.

Plate 26. AUTOMOBILES. *Fig. 1*, Detroit 1907; *Figs. 3-5*, Haynes, 1923; *Fig. 6*, White 1913; *Fig. 7*, Reo 1913.

Plate 27. AUTOMOBILES. *Fig. 1*, Overland 1915; *Fig. 2*, Stanhope 1915; *Fig. 3*, Bell 1921; *Fig. 4*, Packard 1908.

Plate 28. AUTOMOBILES. *Fig. 1*, Chalmers 1909; *Fig. 2*, Studebaker Electric 1903; *Fig. 3*, ca 1895; *Fig. 4*, Ford 1907.

Plate 29. AUTOMOBILES. *Fig. 1*, Ford 1915; *Fig. 2*, Dayton; *Fig. 4*, Franklin 1918.

Plate 30. AUTOMOBILES. *Fig. 1*, Winton 1915; *Fig. 2*, International Harvester 1915; *Fig. 3*, Friedman Road Wagon 1901-2; *Fig. 4*, Herresford 1911.

Plate 31. BIRDS AND FOWL. *Fig. 1*, Bird of Paradise; *Fig. 2*, Flamingo; *Fig. 5*, Barn Owl; *Figs. 6, 7*, Owls; *Fig. 8*, Woodcock; *Fig. 9*, Hawk; *Fig. 10*, Swan; *Fig. 12*, Ostrich; *Fig. 13*, Flamingo.

Plate 33. BIRDS AND FOWL. *Fig. 4*, Peacock; *Fig. 6*, Quail; *Fig. 7*, Auk; *Fig. 8*, Toucan; *Fig. 9*, Robin; *Fig. 10*, Parrot; *Fig. 11*, Avocet.

Plate 34. BIRDS AND FOWL. *Fig. 1*, Wild Turkey; *Fig. 5*, Quail; *Fig. 6*, Hawk; *Fig. 7*, Woodpecker; *Fig. 8*, Canary; *Fig. 9*, Swan; *Fig. 10*, Baltimore Oriole.

Plate 35. BIRDS AND FOWL. *Fig. 1*, Dove; *Fig. 2*, Wren; *Fig. 3*, Pheasant; *Fig. 4*, Heron; *Figs. 6, 10*, Owl; *Fig. 8*, Pigeon.

Plate 46. CHRISTMAS. *Fig. 1* by Thomas Nast.

Plate 47. CHRISTMAS. *Figs. 1, 3* by Tomas Nast.

Plate 48. CHRISTMAS. *Figs. 1, 5* by Thomas Nast.

Plate 50. CHRISTMAS. *Fig. 3* by Thomas Nast.

Plate 52. CHRISTMAS. *Figs. 1-4, 6-8* reproduced through the courtesy of the New York Historical Society (Landauer Collection); *Fig. 5* by Thomas Nast.

Plate 53. CHRISTMAS. *Figs. 1-3, 5-8* reproduced through the courtesy of the New York Historical Society (Landauer Collection); *Fig. 4* by Thomas Nast.

Plate 54. CHRISTMAS. *Fig. 1* by Thomas Nast; *Figs. 2, 4, 7* reproduced through the courtesy of the New York Historical Society (Landauer Collection).

Notes for Plates 103 through 115 prepared by Paul H. Downing.

Plate 103. HORSE DRAWN VEHICLES. *Fig. 1*, Horse-Car or Street-Car, the type used in New York City from 1845 until early 20th century; *Fig. 2*, "Double-decker" horse drawn R.R. car, mid 19th century; *Fig. 3*, Covered Wagon, early 19th century.

Plate 104. HORSE DRAWN VEHICLES. *Fig. 1*, Family Sleigh and Pair, 2nd half 19th century; *Fig. 2*, Albany Cutters and Family sleigh, 2nd half 19th century; *Fig. 3*, Ice Wagon, 1860-1910; *Fig. 4*, Coal Cart Dumping, 2nd half 19th century; *Fig. 5*, Barouche or Calash and Pair, about 1850; *Fig. 6*, Extension Top Phaeton, about 1860; *Fig. 7*, Coach and Pair, early 19th century, coachman on box, footman standing on hind platform; *Fig. 8*, Wagon, 19th century; *Fig. 9*, Stage Coach, early 19th century; *Fig. 10*, Runabout, 2nd half 19th century; *Fig. 11*, Coal-box Buggy (from the shape of the back of the body), 2nd half 19th century; *Fig. 12*, Trotting race with high wheel Sulkies, 2nd and 3rd quarters 19th century; *Fig. 13*, Albany Cutter, 2nd half 19th century; *Fig. 14*, Ice Wagon, 1860-1910; *Fig. 15*, Calash Coach and Barouche or Calash, 2nd half 19th century; *Fig. 16*, Coal Cart in motion; *Fig. 17*, Landau for State Occasions, 1st half 19th century.

Plate 105. HORSE DRAWN VEHICLES. *Fig. 1*, Park Drag, Four-in-hand coach, sometimes called a "Tally-ho";

Fig. 2, Farm or Work Wagon with removable body; *Fig. 3*, Conestoga Wagon, originated in the Conestoga Valley of Pennsylvania during the 2nd half of 18th century, continued in use over a hundred years; *Fig. 4*, Hearse, mid 19th century; *Fig. 5*, Omnibus, 1850 to 1910; *Fig. 6*, Stage Coach, early 19th century.

Plate 106.   HORSE DRAWN VEHICLES. *Fig. 1*, Victoria (panel-boot type), a popular lady's carriage from 1775-1910; *Figs. 2, 3*, Landaulet, closed and open, the "convertible" of 1760-1910.

Plate 107.   HORSE DRAWN VEHICLES. *Fig. 1*, Berlin Coach and Pair, coachman and groom on the box; *Fig. 2*, Park Drag, the Four-in-hand coach of Society from 1775 to 1920. It was popular for driving to the races or other out of door sporting events, and was erroneously called a "Tally-ho" by the *hoi polloi*.

Plate 108.   HORSE DRAWN VEHICLES. *Fig. 1*, Vis-à-vis, late 19th-early 20th century; *Fig. 2*, Physician's Phaeton, 1875-1910.

Plate 109.   HORSE DRAWN VEHICLES. *Fig. 1*, Victoria Sleigh, late 19th century-early 20th century; *Fig. 2*, Express Wagon, 1850-1910; *Fig. 3*, Stage Coach, mid 19th century; *Fig. 4*, Tandem driving. Not as easy at it looks. Indulged in by sporting men throughout the 19th century.

Plate 110.   HORSE DRAWN VEHICLES. *Fig. 1*, Barouche, presented to General Lafayette by the Congress in 1824; *Fig. 2*, Skeleton Wagon, 2nd half 19th century used in trotting races; *Fig. 3*, Spider Phaeton, 1870-1910, an American carriage which found favor with our English cousins; *Fig. 4*, Concord Wagon, 2nd half 19th century.

Plate 111.   HORSE DRAWN VEHICLES. *Fig. 1*, Rockaway, 1860-1880; *Fig. 2*, Milk Delivery Wagon, 1875-1910.

Plate 112.   HORSE DRAWN VEHICLES. *Fig. 1*, Chaise, 1800-1880. This is the type of Oliver Wendell Holmes' "One-hoss Shay"; *Fig. 2*, Cut-under Basket Phaeton, 1880-1910, popular for lady's driving, the rumble or "dickey" seat was for the groom; *Fig. 3*, Buggy called "Jenny Lind" in honor of the great singer's visit to this country in 1855.

Plate 113. HORSE DRAWN VEHICLES. *Fig. 1*, Hearse, middle to late 19th century; *Fig. 2*, Stage Coach, early 19th century; *Figs. 3, 4*, Horse-Car or Street-Car, the type used in New York City from 1845 until early 20th century; *Fig. 5*, Improved Business Wagon, 1850-1900; *Fig. 6*, Mule-drawn Cotton Wagon, 19th century: *Fig. 7*, Surrey; *Fig. 8*, Stage Coach, nicknamed "The Football Coach" from the shape of the body, early 19th century.

Plate 114.   HORSE DRAWN VEHICLES. *Fig. 1*, Cart with mule or ass, 19th century; *Fig. 2*, Wagon, 1850-1910; *Fig. 3*, Horse-Car or Street-Car, 1832-1850; *Figs. 4, 5*,

Horse and Cart, 19th century; *Fig. 6*, Coach and Chaise, early 19th century; *Fig. 7*, Runabout and Horse, 1860-1890; *Fig. 8*, Conestoga Wagon; *Fig. 9*, Coal Wagon raised by a hand crank to "shoot" its load, 2nd half 19th century and early 20th century; *Figs. 10, 11*, Coach, early 19th century; *Fig. 12*, Omnibus operating on Broadway, New York, 2nd quarter 19th century; *Fig. 13*, Gig, 19th century; *Fig. 14*, Coach, early 19th century; *Fig. 15*, Butcher's Cart, 1850-1910.

Plate 115.   HORSE DRAWN VEHICLES. *Fig. 1*, Jump-seat Barouche, 1860-1880. Carriage arranged with single seat for two passengers; *Fig. 2*, The same carriage with seats rearranged so that it may accommodate four passengers.

Plate 150.   PORTRAITS. *Fig. 1*, Andrew Jackson.

Plate 152.   PORTRAITS. *Fig. 1*, U. S. Grant; *Fig. 4*, Columbus; *Fig. 5*, Shakespeare; *Fig. 6*, William T. Sherman.

Plate 153.   REPTILES, FISH, INSECTS. *Fig. 1*, Queen honeybee; *Fig. 2*, Drone honeybee; *Fig. 3*, Worker honeybee; *Fig. 4*, Crab; *Fig. 5*, Flea; *Fig. 6*, Marine turtle; *Figs. 7, 8*, Moth; *Fig. 9*, Beetle; *Fig. 10*, Butterfly; *Fig. 11*, Dragonfly; *Fig. 12*, Tussah moth; *Fig. 13*, Housefly; *Fig. 14*, Bluecrab; *Fig. 15*, Diamond back terrapin; *Fig. 16*, Lizzard; *Fig. 17*, Alligator; *Fig. 18*, Rattlesnake; *Fig. 19*, Sea robin; *Fig. 20*, Cowrie shell.

Plate 154.   REPTILES, FISH, INSECTS. *Fig. 1*, Shrimp; *Fig. 2*, Crayfish; *Fig. 3*, Pike; *Fig. 4*, Weakfish; *Fig. 5*, Herring; *Fig. 6*, Oyster; *Fig. 9*, Porgy; *Fig. 10*, Frog; *Fig. 11*, Cod; *Fig. 12*, Sea turtle; *Fig. 13*, Box turtle; *Fig. 14*, Lobster; *Fig. 15*, Crocodile; *Fig. 16*, Crab; *Fig. 17*, Scorpion.

Plate 178.   SYMBOLS AND EMBLEMS. *Fig. 1*, Knights of Golden Eagle; *Fig. 2*, United States; *Fig. 6*, New Jersey; *Fig. 7*, Pennsylvania; *Fig. 9*, Sons of St. George; *Fig. 10*, New York.

Plate 179.   SYMBOLS AND EMBLEMS. *Fig. 1*, Argentina; *Fig. 2*, South Carolina; *Fig. 3*, New York; *Fig. 4*, Masonic; *Fig. 5*, Missouri.

Plate 180.   SYMBOLS AND EMBLEMS. *Fig. 1*, Florida; *Fig. 2*, Foresters; *Fig. 3*, Nevada; *Fig. 4*, Peru; *Fig. 5*, Argentina; *Fig. 7*, Massachusetts; *Fig. 9*, Order of Red Men.

Plate 181. SYMBOLS AND EMBLEMS. *Fig. 2*, Portugal; *Fig. 3*, Peru.

Plate 182.   SYMBOLS AND EMBLEMS. *Figs. 6, 9-15*, Masonic; *Fig. 8*, Elks.

Plate 183.   SYMBOLS AND EMBLEMS. *Figs. 1-3*, Odd Fellows; *Fig. 4*, Mexico; *Fig. 6*, Temple of Honor; *Fig. 7*, Grand Army of the Republic; *Fig. 8*, Foresters.

The major sources of illustrations are type specimen books prior to 1890. Because the illustrations appear frequently in different catalogues and different years, the publisher believes that no useful or scholarly purpose is served by giving the exact source since no effort was made to reproduce or investigate their first appearance.

The following specimen catalogues were the main sources for this collection:

MacKellar, Smiths and Jordan.

White, John T. NEW YORK TYPE FOUNDRY SPECIMEN OF PRINTING TYPES CAST.

A. Zeese and Company.

James Conner's Sons.

Blomgren and Co.

Phelps Dalton and Co.

The following sources were also used:

Scrapbooks of the works of Dr. Alexander Anderson in the New York Public Library.

BALLOU'S PICTORIAL DRAWING-ROOM COMPANION.

HORSELESS AGE.

The Landauer Collection in the New York Historical Society.

THOMAS NAST'S CHRISTMAS DRAWINGS OF THE HUMAN RACE. Harper and Bros. 1890.

The plates of Trade Advertisements were taken from

AMERICAN PORTRAIT GALLERY, 1855

ILLUSTRATED AMERICAN ADVERTISER, 1856

The following check-list from the catalogue files of the Typographic Library of Columbia University, New York, represents the most complete collection of specimen books in America. The volumes were gathered by the late Henry Lewis Bullen, acting as curator and collector for the American Type Founders Company.

ALBANY TYPE FOUNDRY, R. Starr & Co., 1826.

BALTIMORE TYPE FOUNDRY, (Fielding Lucas, Jr.,
         agent) 1832.
"   "   "   F. Lucas, 1851.
"   "   "   Lucas Brothers, 1854.
"   "   "   H. L. Pelouze & Son,
         1879.

BINNEY & RONALDSON, Philadelphia, 1809.
"   "   "   1812.

JAMES RONALDSON,   Philadelphia, 1816
"   "   "   1822.

BOSTON TYPE FOUNDRY, 1820.
"   "   "   1825.
"   "   "   1826, (John Rogers, agent)
"   "   "   1828.
"   "   "   1832.
"   "   "   1837.
"   "   "   1845.
"   "   "   John K. Rogers&Co., 1853.

"   "   "   John K. Rogers&Co., 1856.
"   "   "   "   "   "   1857.
"   "   "   "   "   "   1860.
"   "   "   "   "   "   1864.
"   "   "   "   "   "   1867.
"   "   "   "   "   "   1869.
"   "   "   "   "   "   1871.

BOSTON TYPE FOUNDRY, John K. Rogers&Co., 1874.
"   "   "   "   "   " c. 1875.
"   "   "   "   "   "   1878.
"   "   "   "   "   "   1880.
"   "   "   "   "   "   1883.

BRUCE, DAVID & GEORGE, New York, 1815.
"   "   "   "   "   1815-16.
"   "   "   "   "   1818.

CHANDLER, A., New York, 1822.

CINCINNATI TYPE FOUNDRY, O. & H. Wells, 1827.
"   "   "   "   "   1834.
"   "   "   (Horace Wells,
         agent)   1844.
"   "   "   (L. T. Wells,
         agent)   1851.
"   "   "   "   "   1852.
"   "   "   "   " c. 1853.
"   "   "   "   "   1856.

CONNER & COOKE, New York, 1834.
"   "   "   "   1836.
"   "   "   "   1837.
"   "   (Supplement to the 1836 book)

JAMES CONNER & SON, New York, 1841.
"   "   "   "   "   1850.
"   "   "   "   "   1852.
"   "   "   "   "   before 1855.
"   "   "   "   "   1855.
"   "   "   "   "   1859.
"   "   "   "   "   1860.
         1870.
"   "   "   "   "   1876.
"   "   "   "   "   1885.
"   "   "   "   "   1888.
"   "   "   "   "   1891.

DICKENSON TYPE FOUNDRY, (Samuel N. Dicken-
         son) Boston, 1842.
"   "   "   (Samuel N. Dicken-
         son) Boston, 1847.
"   "   "   (Phelps and Dalton)
         Boston, 1855.

FRANKLIN TYPE FOUNDRY, Allison, Smith & Johnson,
         Cincinnati, 1871.
"   "   "   "   1873.

FRANKLIN LETTER-FOUNDRY, A. W. Kinsley &
         Company, Albany, 1829.

HAGAR, WILLIAM & CO., New York, 1826.
"   "   "   "   "   1831.
"   "   "   "   "   1841.
"   "   "   "   "   1850
"   "   "   "   "   1854.
"   "   "   "   "   1858.
"   "   "   "   "   1860.
"   "   "   "   "   1873.
"   "   "   "   "   1886.

JOHNSON & SMITH, Phila., 1834.
      (Successors to Binney and Ronaldson
 " " " 1841.
 " " " 1843.

LAWRENCE JOHNSON, Philadelphia, 1844
 " " " c. 1845.

LAWRENCE JOHNSON & CO., Phila., 1847.
 " " " " 1849.
 " " " " before 1853.
 " " " " 1853.
 " " " " 1856.
 " " " " 1857.
 " " " " 1859.
 " " " " 1865.

MAC KELLAR, SMITHS & JORDAN, Phila., 1868.
 " " " " 1869.
 " " " " 1871.
 " " " " 1873.
 " " " " 1876.
 " " " " 1877.
 " " " " 1878.
 " " " " 1881.
 " " " " 1882.
 " " " " 1884.
 " " " " 1885.
 " " " " 1886.
 " " " " 1887.
 " " " " 1888.

MAC KELLAR, SMITHS & JORDAN, Phila., 1889.
 " " " " 1890.
 " " " " 1892.
 " " " " 1894.

MAC KELLAR, SMITHS & JORDAN, Phila.,1895.
 " " " " 1897.

LOTHIAN, GEORGE B., New York, 1841.

LYMAN, NATHAN & COMPANY, Buffalo, 1841.
 " " " " 1853.

NEW ENGLAND TYPE FOUNDRY, Henry Willis,
        Boston, 1834.
 " " " " George and J.
        Curtis,
        Boston, 1838.
 " " " " 1841.

OHIO TYPE FOUNDRY, Guilford & Jones,
        Cincinnati, 1851.

PELOUZE, LEWIS, Philadelphia, 1849.

PELOUZE, LEWIS & SON, Philadelphia, 1856.

REICH, STARR & COMPANY, Philadelphia, 1818.

ROBB & ECKLIN, Philadelphia, 1836.

ALEXANDER ROBB, Philadelphia, 1844.

STARR & LITTLE, Albany, 1828.

WHITE, ELIHU, New York, 1812.
 " " " " 1817.
 " " " " 1821.
 " " " " 1826.
 " " " " 1829.

Numbers in boldface refer to pages and numbers following slash refer to specific figures on the page.